Overcoming Bride

Requests for information should be directed to:
Tara Browder Media
tarabrowdermedia@gmail.com

ISBN-13: 978-1517209933
ISBN-10: 1517209935

*Thank you to Colleen Kimball of Technicraft in Peoria, IL for cover copy design and Sej Baur (freelance illustrator) of Austin, TX for cover art design.

Endorsements

WOW!!! I just finished reading Tara's book in two sittings. It was a beautiful mixture of the profound and the light-hearted. Tara invites us into the deepest places in her heart to see a glimpse of how God met her in her pain and in her longing. She is authentic, whimsical and real. It's as if she is sitting right beside you sharing her story and inviting you into God's personal story for you. It deeply touched my heart and gave me a greater longing to know God as my bridegroom and give Him anything that stands in the way of knowing Him in full intimacy. Prepare to be moved, challenged, encouraged, and filled with hope.

---Karin Harper, Grow Pastor
Gateway Church Austin, TX

Overcoming Bride is an intimate look into the life of a passionate follower of Jesus Christ. It opens a door into the heart of God toward His people, welcoming weary travelers to find rest within. Tara writes in a way that is both personal and universal; she shows us the way for her story to become *our* stories. Her God is our God, Lord of heaven and earth and Romancer of our hearts.

---Reverend Sarah Ago M.A. Family Life Education
Pastor of Compassion, Justice, and Missions
Hillside Covenant Church
Walnut Creek, CA

Tara shares her story in such an authentic way and helps us understand the ways that God can use our most difficult moments to reveal His goodness and His pursuit of us.

> **---Dr. Eric Michael Bryant, Campus Pastor**
> **Gateway Church Austin, TX**
> **Author of *Not Like Me: A Field Guide for***
> ***Influencing a Diverse World***

Dedication

This is for You, Jesus.

Thank You for Being my Savior and

the Greatest Romancer of my heart.

Acknowledgement

Thank you to all my friends and family for your constant support in my life-long journey to knowing Jesus more deeply and living from a place of victory. Also, a special thank you to those who spent endless hours helping to edit, market, design, and publish <u>Overcoming Bride</u>. This book and release of the message within would not have been possible without you.

Table of Contents

Foreword

Overcoming Bride is an intimate look into the life of a passionate follower of Jesus Christ. It opens a door into the heart of God toward His people, welcoming weary travelers to find rest within. Tara writes in a way that is both personal and universal; she shows us the way for her story to become *our* stories. Her God is our God, Lord of heaven and earth and Romancer of our hearts.

It has been said that our greatest ministry is produced through our greatest pain. One definitely sees the truth in that statement through the life of Tara Browder. As her friend, many times I have wanted to say "enough" to the pain that she has endured! Take any one difficulty that she has walked through and it would be plenty. Yet, Tara has overcome again and again. It is to God's glory that she continues to minister with power and great hope.

I remember her Skype call vividly in February of 2013- Tara was calling to tell me that she was engaged. I was sitting in a hotel room in Thailand and I could hardly believe my ears. I felt so happy for her; delighted that FINALLY her season had come. I was ready to walk the aisle as a bridesmaid and take the arm of her brother. My son was going to be her ring bearer and we were planning our trip to the wedding. Just two months later, my heart sank and my eyes filled with tears as I heard her tell me that everything was called off. The thought of this loss happening to her was simply too much.

A few weeks later, we sat together on a beach in Mendocino, California, praying and weeping. We watched the waves crash over and over onto the shore and we were reminded of the faithfulness of God to keep coming to us, time and time again. There were no answers as to why this had happened or how to fix it. There was only the comfort of sitting in the pain together in the presence of God.

I had watched Tara move victoriously through loss before. I remember running up her driveway the night I found out that her mother had gone to be with Jesus and embracing her in shared grief. I will never forget watching her minister through a choreographed dance at her mother's funeral a few days later. I was amazed that she had the strength to honor her through dancing to the song, "His Eye is on the Sparrow." She praised her mother's Maker in a beautiful dance of remembrance and hope.

As she faced the loss of her upcoming marriage, I knew that once again she would make it through excruciating pain. I ached to see her lose someone else who was so precious to her. Her engagement represented the fulfillment of great promise. How could this be taken away?

I still don't know the answers to all of the "whys" but I have had a front row seat to the redemption God continues to bring in Tara's life. He has taken her brokenness and built lives up from it. He has reached into her despair and given her a message of hope for others. He has removed her agony and replaced it with deep, lasting joy. He has taken the sacrifice of praise that Tara offered and abundantly blessed it.

Tara's ministry is an example of David's beautiful statement of worship in 2 Samuel 24:24 when he said, "I will not offer burnt offerings to the Lord my God that cost me nothing." Tara's offerings have been more costly than most, but she has given them freely and fully. You will see the fruit of those gifts described throughout this book.

I encourage you to read her words slowly, reflecting and digesting the powerful biblical principles that Tara teaches through. Look at the stories from Scripture with fresh vision. I believe that the most important truth you can glean from this book is that God does not waste an ounce of our pain, but redeems it fully. Hold tightly to this hope!

You will be blessed by walking a few miles with Tara. May you know the depth of God's love and mercy in your life as you read of His passionate love in her own journey.

Rev. Sarah Ago
Pastor of Compassion, Justice and Missions
Hillside Covenant Church
Walnut Creek, CA

Introduction

This book is not just about love and loss. It's about overcoming and bearing fruit in our lives no matter the season. It reveals the rawness of the heart and the journey through and out of grief. It testifies of God's justice and the redeeming power of His love. Going through a broken engagement or being a woman is NOT a prerequisite for reading this book! In fact, no matter your gender or your history, when you become a follower and believer in Christ, you instantly become a bride---His Bride. Here are just a few scriptures that mention this:

Isaiah 54:5 "For your Maker is your husband, the Lord of hosts is his name; and the Holy One of Israel is your Redeemer, the God of the whole earth he is called."

Ephesians 5:25-30 "Husbands, love your wives, as Christ loved the church and gave himself up for her, that he might sanctify her, having cleansed her by the washing of water with the word, so that he might present the church to himself in splendor, without spot or wrinkle or any such thing, that she might be holy and without blemish. In the same way husbands should love their wives as their own bodies. He who loves his wife loves himself. For no one ever hated his own flesh, but nourishes and cherishes it, just as Christ does the church, because we are members of his body."

Revelation 19:7-9 "Let us rejoice and exult and give him the glory, for the marriage of the Lamb has come, and his Bride has made herself ready; it was granted her to clothe herself with fine linen, bright and pure—for the fine linen is the righteous deeds of the saints. And the angel said to me, 'Write this: Blessed are those who are invited to the marriage supper of the Lamb.' And he said to me, 'These are the true words of God.'"

Are you a man or woman who desires to rekindle your relationship with God?

Are you looking for hope through a fresh testimony of God's justice and redemption?

Are you needing encouragement and strength in the wilderness?

Are you a man or woman who needs some fresh perspective on God's heart regarding relationships between men and women?

Are you married but finding yourself disillusioned because you are still lacking the depth of love you had hoped to find on the other side of marriage?

Are you single or dating and still trying to find the balance between believing for a Godly spouse and finding all of your fulfillment in Jesus?

Have you gone through a broken engagement, divorce, or death of a loved one and need encouragement during grieving?

Are you wondering if grief and seasons in the wilderness have an expiration date?

If you answered "Yes" to any of these questions, this book is written with you in mind. I pray that my story of how God led me through the wilderness of a broken engagement will help you live as a constantly OVERCOMING and VICTORIOUS Bride!!!

__Chapter One__

Whirlwind Romance

Other than one extremely awkward blind date to break up the
monotony of my singlehood, nothing surfaced on the romance
radar during all of my twenties and most of my thirties. But my
singlehood was getting ready to get a swift kick in the gut on
February 13, 2013. That's the day he surprised me with roses.

Who's he? One of my best friends for over a decade. Sure, we had
the "define-the-relationship" talks over that decade, but they
always ended with fresh reminders that we were "just friends." I
had always loved him. I met him shortly after my mother passed
away in 1999. During one of the most painful seasons of my life up
to that point, he was a light in the midst of the darkness. The
trauma of that season blotted out much of my memory of the first
year without my mom, but I could always remember in vivid detail
the moments I spent with him----the walks, the meals together,
late night trips to the movie theatre or driving around town. And

how can I forget all the laughter? We always made each other laugh.

Even with all this chemistry, I settled in to knowing what I assumed our relationship would never be. When you know you will always be "just friends," something tells you to reserve that love for someone else one day, and you tuck it away deep in your heart for safe keeping. After thirteen years, I subconsciously got into a pattern of ignoring any feelings of romantic love and just enjoying the friendship with him. That was until I received the shock of my life the day before Valentine's Day in 2013. I was attending a conference in his town, and I arrived at my hotel one evening to find roses had been delivered to my room. I assumed I was somehow in the wrong room and glanced around to get my bearings. I quickly realized my luggage was right where I stored it earlier in the day, and that the flowers on the desk belonged to me. I sat and shook from head to toe on the edge of my bed as I stared at that vase of flowers for ten minutes. I knew who delivered them. He was the only man I knew in that town.

In that moment, all the love I subconsciously stuffed into an attic or basement of my heart for all those years suddenly materialized front and center. I had chosen him long before he had chosen me. The dust was being blown off of that love as it was resurfacing from where it had been stored. After reading the card attached to the flowers, gazing at the vase a little longer, and taking the time to take a selfie of me with the roses, I called him.

Yes, I took a selfie. Why? I never wanted to forget what this moment felt like. It had been so long since I felt chosen, wanted, and desired at this level by anyone other than God. Plus, I knew the cost for him to give me those flowers. Yes, roses are sold at a premium on and around Valentine's Day, but I'm not talking about the monetary cost. I was fully aware of the real price he paid to give me those flowers—the price to let go of fear in order to gain love.

I loved and respected him more that day than I ever had because I knew the blockade of fear he had to surmount just to reveal how he felt about me. I called him and gushed as I thanked him for the flowers. He asked me when we could see each other, and I said, "Right now!", even though "right now" was almost midnight. I couldn't wait to hug him and see his face, but we decided to go on our first date on Valentine's Day and that he would pick me up early the next morning.

I didn't sleep one bit that night. The excitement and also the fear of entering into a romance with such a longtime friend overwhelmed me. Fearful of the unknown, my solace was that I would walk this upcoming journey with God and one of my best friends, who would soon become my boyfriend. The hours of the night slowly advanced, and I finally emerged from my bed to get ready for my Valentine's early morning arrival.

It felt so natural to be his girlfriend, and I was basking in the beauty of fresh romance. Just a few days later, he unexpectedly said, "So, when are we going to get married?" In no way at the time did I think: *Whoah! This is going too fast. I'm not sure about this.* Because I had loved him and known him for over a decade, the same question had bounced around in my heart a few times in the first three days of our romance. So, I answered his question with a, "I'll leave that up to you."

The next day, it was clear, he planned on wasting no time. After a drive to a waterfall, and his asking how long it would take me to plan a wedding, the date was set, and we called my grandparents to begin officially announcing our whirlwind of a romance and future wedding. Our hearts were connected. We savored each moment of holding hands and walking together at the waterfall that day. Even though the air was chilled and the waterfall was actually part gargantuan icicle, we sat nearby on a park bench together wrapped in a blanket that he brought for the occasion.

After this, we immediately went into wedding planning mode. In no way did this seem rushed to me. We had known each other for so long, and we had always wanted to marry someone we considered to be our best friend. I was in my mid-thirties and he was in his late forties, so we saw no reason to purposely delay a wedding. The pace of getting married in six months seemed totally reasonable at the time.

I experienced all the bliss that future brides cherish. The day at the bridal salon picking out a dress amid tears of joy and laughter with close friends and family. Registering for wedding gifts with my future groom. Receiving my wedding dress in the mail, trying it on, and dreaming of the day I would get to walk down the aisle to a man I deeply loved. Engagement parties, telling the story of our relationship repeatedly to friends and family and setting dates for bridal showers. It never got old telling that story, and entering a time of romance and celebration after such a long stint of singleness was more than welcome.

Never in my wildest imagination did I ever think that this pure romance would end as quickly as it began, and that a little under two months from the moment by the waterfall, I would be unexpectedly thrust into planning for a "funeral" instead of a wedding. I had known loss, but never grief like this. Without much explanation, one of my best friends for over a decade—my future groom-- through tears and much pain told me on a Skype call that he could not marry me.

I was in shock. I failed to see this coming. I was flooded with a million thoughts at once. *Did I hurt him? Did I not love him and cherish him well? Is this my fault? Maybe there is something wrong with me. After all, I had not even been on a date for seventeen years before him. Am I toxic to men? How am I going to tell my family and friends? Maybe he will change his mind. We are friends, so surely we can work this out. How do I fix this? What does he need right now? God, what should I say to him right now?*

The final question was the only one answered. I heard God say, "Tell him you love him. That's all there is to say right now." So, I obeyed. I said, "I love you" and asked him what we should do now since he was silent at this point. He told me I was his best friend and that he couldn't hang up on me, so I said, "I love you" again and reluctantly submitted my "goodbye" before hanging up.

I reached out to him several times in the year following that Skype call. I longed to understand what went wrong. If I had hurt him in any way, I wanted to make it right, and I expressed that the best I knew how. I was only met with silence, and I wondered if I was even texting or calling a number that still existed. The silence crippled my heart and nearly crushed my spirit. The walk through grief was just beginning, and I found that I missed our friendship more than anything.

One thing I can say for certain about that time is that my fiancée left that day, but Jesus never did. My fiancé was silent, but God's voice rang out in the midst of that arid place of quiet. Ironically, in a time when I felt more like a widow than a bride, God was about to propose to me Himself, and take me on a journey of healing and romance beyond my wildest dreams.

Chapter Two

Woman vs. Lawn Mower

I was aware of what it cost my fiancée to admit his love for me, but I was also all too mindful of how expensive it was for me to express my love for him. I wasn't always open to men. In fact, early on in my life, I had seeds of distrust, disrespect, and even hatred toward men planted in my heart as a result of my experiences and disappointments. Those seeds germinated, took root, and weaved a garden of weeds in my heart throughout my childhood, teen years, and into my twenties and early thirties. It wasn't until late 2010 and early 2011 that I realized just how much those weeds had overtaken my heart.

How did these weeds manifest in my day-to-day interactions with men? I made a vow that I would never need a man, and most importantly, I would never allow them to know they affected me. I withheld affirmation from my brothers in Christ. I refused their help when they wanted to help me carry something and felt uncomfortable when they opened a door for me. I secretly, and many times unknowingly, judged them as weak, less spiritual, and less capable than women. I expected them to abandon me or fail me when I needed them most, and I rarely anticipated goodness from them. I viewed them as selfish and fickle, and if they did anything that impressed me, I quickly reminded myself not to count on that lasting long.

My expectations of my brothers in Christ and fathers who God placed in my life were unrealistic. I expected them to be only what God could be, and when they failed, I became harder and harder in my heart towards them. Since most of these feelings remained under the surface and rarely manifested in vivid display for others, few who knew me would have said, "Tara is a man-hater!" However, if I am honest in looking back, anger and pain related to men were ever brewing under the surface of my heart, always threatening to erupt at an inopportune time.

The story I am about to share, although humorous, paints a picture of how I operated during the time in my life before God began to gently and graciously remove the weeds of my pain and hate. I had just bought a house in Charlotte, North Carolina, and for reasons unknown, I had failed to realize that, as a homeowner, I would need a lawn mower. It wasn't until I received several notices from the homeowners association about my tall grass and how I needed to cut my lawn, that it dawned on me the importance of owning one.

So, out of fear of not complying with the homeowners association, I visited my local Wal-Mart to purchase a lawn mower. To my surprise, the lawn mowers were enclosed in a box, and they needed to be assembled by the owner. As I approached the checkout counter, I reassured myself by thinking---*How hard can it be to assemble a lawn mower?*

It was then that my male cashier asked me this most "threatening" question: "Would you like us to assemble the lawn mower for you? It's only $10 more if you would like us to assemble it." I promptly and arrogantly responded, "Do I look like someone who can't put a lawn mower together?" I was insulted. Who was this man who assumed that I could not assemble a lawn mower? I barked out "No thank you!" after which, he graciously said, "No problem, ma'am. Just make sure you have these two types of screwdrivers and wrenches when you put it together."

Because I had assumed all the tools would be included in the box, this was information I needed, but I wasn't about to apologize for my arrogance. Thanks to my dad who taught me a few things about tools, I knew the difference between a Phillips and standard screwdriver, but unfortunately, I didn't own either. I asked the cashier to wait for me as I scurried back to the tool department to grab the necessary items for my project.

The tools cost more than the $10 assembly fee, but I wasn't trying to save money. I had something to prove to this cashier at Wal-Mart. I had to prove I was just as capable as he was. He needed to know that I wasn't weak and that I didn't need his help. Even though I would probably never see him again, I needed to know that I had "won," and I needed to further sustain my belief that I did not need a man.

I loaded my lawn mower into my Honda Civic and zipped home for a short sleep before the alarm clock buzzed in the early morning hours, waking me up for my project. I needed to assemble the lawn mower so it was functional before the hot summer sun blared down mercilessly.

After opening the box, I realized the only instructions were in French. I still forged ahead in my battle to prove myself and improvised by using the pictures. After six grueling hours assembling this lawn mower in my living room, I was still struggling with the last step of assembly---attaching a wire to the throttle on the handle bar of the push mower. My stubborn self insisted on completing the task, and even after six hours of fatiguing assembly work, the thought of calling Wal-Mart and asking for help felt like miserable defeat. I imagined my cashier from the previous night answering the phone and laughing diabolically while celebrating his victory.

Yet, in the throws of it all, I buckled and caved. I fell to my knees in my kitchen, and I wept and hit the floor with my fists. Along with a few expletives coming out of my mouth, I yelled toward heaven---"If You (God) had only given me a husband by now, this lawn mower would have been assembled!!!"

Leave it to moments of defeat or frustration to reveal the truth of the heart. As difficult as it was to admit under normal conditions, I desired a man in my life, and I wanted to need a man. It was in this moment of weakness that I called Wal-Mart. After an unsuccessful hour-long conversation with an employee in the lawn and garden department trying to help me complete the last step of assembly over the phone, he welcomed me to bring the lawn mower back to the store where he would complete the assembly process for free.

However, there was a slight problem. At this point, I would have to disassemble and destroy the work I had already mastered in order to fit it into my Honda Civic. With a broken spirit, I began to cry and the worker on the other end of the phone said, "Please don't cry, ma'am. My girlfriend can't put things together very well either. That's why I help her." Normally, I would have been insulted by such discourse, but in this moment, I actually saw them as comforting words being given to an undeserving woman. It was endearing that he didn't want me to cry. I thanked him for his kindness and hung up.

At this point, the real test ensued. Because there was no way I could fit the fully assembled mower into my car to return it to Wal-Mart, I knew that I would now have to walk to my neighbor's house and look a man in the eye and ask for his help. Here I was at 3 o'clock in the afternoon wearing a sweaty t-shirt and shorts and looking like a grease monkey. And I was about to admit that a lawn mower and, ultimately, the Wal-Mart cashier from the night before defeated me.

My neighbor immediately came to my rescue. What had taken me hours to fail to figure out took him twenty seconds to accomplish. He popped that wire into the throttle with ease, unknowingly making me feel even more like a fool, but I was thankful. Then, as he stood up and looked at my disheveled self, he knew it was only right to offer to mow the lawn. Part of me wanted to say, "No!", but the other part of me was yelling "SHUT UP!!! Enough already!!! Let the man help you!" I listened to the latter, and, as a result, my homeowners association and I were the better for it.

My lawn mower adventure is a humorous yet telling revelation of how my heart was postured toward most men until God healed me. A major milestone in that healing happened in 2011. I was in class at a school of ministry, and we started every class day with worship. I was singing along, and suddenly, I heard God say very clearly, "Go over to Caleb and ask him for a hug." I ignored this and pawned it off as ridiculous. I said to God, "Why should I ask Caleb for a hug when You can give me a hug? I just need a hug from You."

In order to know how ridiculous it was for me to disobey God's instructions, you have to know about Caleb. Caleb is someone I would describe as being "without guile." He was one of those guys who liked to hug everyone, and he reminded me of how kind Jesus is. He was safe. He was pure. He was engaged to a precious woman, and I didn't have to worry about him thinking I had some type of ulterior motive with him. Yet, even though I knew those things, I thought it was utterly insane that God would ask me to request a hug from Caleb. I had a hard enough time asking for help with a lawn mower. Asking for a hug was taking things to a whole new level!

God and I argued for a while, and He said, "Tara, you need this (the hug). I want you to trust men. I want you to need and want men in your life." God wasn't meaning "need" in a codependent way, but when He used the word "need," He might as well have said, "Be subservient," or "Admit weakness," or "Be codependent," according to my heart's filter. However, He was really saying, "Be humble," "Be loved," "Be comforted," and "Experience the hug of a brother." He was telling me that if I only felt safe with moms and sisters, but failed to be vulnerable with fathers and brothers, I was missing out on something I needed---a unique expression of His heart that is revealed through the masculine.

I eventually obeyed, and fearfully walked over to Caleb. I said, "Caleb, God told me to ask you for a hug. I am embarrassed, but I want to obey Him." Right then, Caleb smiled and said, "Of course!" He gently pulled me into a hug and cradled the back of my head with his hand. He whispered to me, "Tara, you need this." It was then- the moment Caleb echoed God's exact words to me -that I broke. I cried for a few minutes, and then the hug ended.

I failed to realize then how much that one moment would alter my life. In as much as that hug changed me, the act of asking for that hug reversed a vicious cycle. Asking for that hug shattered a pattern in my life, and it broke a vow I had made long before to never need a man. There are some vows that are meant to be broken because they were never supposed to be established in the first place. The vow that I made to never need a man was one of them.

Sometimes God might ask us to do something that we think is utterly ridiculous, but when we obey, healing is on the other side of that obedience. Remember Naaman? His story is told in 2 Kings 5:1-14:

> Naaman, commander of the army of the king of Syria, was a great man with his master and in high favor, because by him the Lord had given victory to Syria. He was a mighty man of valor, but he was leper. Now the Syrians on one of their raids had carried off a little girl from the land of Israel, and she worked in the service of Naaman's wife. She said to her mistress, "Would that my lord were with the prophet who is in Samaria! He would cure him of his leprosy... So Naaman came with his horses and chariots and stood at the door of Elisha's house. And Elisha sent a messenger to him, saying, "Go and wash in the Jordan seven times, and your flesh shall be restored, and you shall be clean." But Naaman was angry and went away, saying, "Behold, I thought that he would surely come out to me and stand and call upon the name of the Lord his God, and wave his hand over the place and cure the leper. Are not Abana and Pharpar, the rivers of Damascus, better than all the waters of Israel? Could I not wash in them and be clean?" So he turned and went away in

a rage. But his servants came near and said to him, "My father, it is a great word the prophet has spoken to you; will you not do it? Has he actually said to you, 'Wash, and be clean'?" So he went down and dipped himself seven times in the Jordan, according to the word of the man of God, and his flesh was restored like the flesh of a little child, and he was clean.

Through the prophet Elisha, God told Naaman that if he wanted to be healed from leprosy, he needed to wash seven times in the Jordan River. Naaman wondered why God couldn't have just allowed him to take a nice, clean rinse in a river closer to his home. He couldn't understand why God was not allowing him to do what he considered most convenient. He was even "angry" and in a "rage" at God because of the healing method that God chose. He was hoping that God would have just healed him directly through the prophet Elisha. However, because Naaman ultimately obeyed God's seemingly ridiculous request, he was healed. Naaman's act of obedience, not a prophet's prayers, led to his healing. I'm sure Naaman was quite grateful that he ultimately overcame his prideful resistance and obeyed God.

Another example of a time when God made a seemingly crazy request, was when He told Joshua and all the Israelites to march around Jericho seven times in order to see the city wall destroyed. As a result of their praise, worship, and obedience, He would cause the wall to crumble (See Joshua 6). God could have just obliterated that wall with one crushing motion of His right hand, but He was after more than the Israelites witnessing another miracle like the Red Sea. He was after their hearts, and He wanted their trust.

Like Naaman and Joshua, I was asked to trust God while obeying what seemed like a foolish request. God knew that my obedience would usher me into an entirely new way of relating to men. Despite how frightening it was to be in that unfamiliar place of needing a man, when I broke the unhealthy vow I made, I noticed an immediate shift in my relationships with men. That week, a man at the grocery store followed me through the produce section just to catch up with me to tell me I was beautiful. I couldn't remember the last time any man approached me like that. Also, in that same week, three brothers in Christ, on separate occasions, approached me and told me that "something" was different about me and that I was glowing and beautiful. One even said, "I am going to be honest. For a long time I thought you didn't like me, but something about you seems different now."

One act of obedience. One choice to need a gender that represents a part of God's image. One step to ask for a hug suddenly shifted something in the spirit and I was approachable to men in an entirely new way. This led me on a journey of repenting for the ways I had reacted to men throughout my life, and this even included how I viewed God.

As part of this healing process, during a worship time at church in January 2013, God spoke to me and said, "I want you to give Me permission to affect you." Honestly, I was offended. Up to that point in my life, I had experienced much with God. I knew His embrace, and He taught me who He is as my father and my husband. However, it was clear in His request that I had only experienced Him this way in part of my heart but not fully. God didn't just want a condo on the east side of my heart; He wanted all of the real estate. He wanted to stretch out and make Himself at home in me, but He wanted my permission to do that.

When the God of the universe asks for all of you, you give Him all of you. After all, He gave us all of Himself. So, in that moment, during worship, I whispered to God, "I give you permission to affect me." Immediately, I felt the weight of God's presence rest upon me, and I could no longer stand. I fell to my knees and then to my face and was glued to the floor for about thirty minutes. I wept as wave upon wave of His tangible love washed over me, and I began to experience what I had been protecting myself from all through the years.

In the coming days, I experienced God in ways I had never imagined possible. He felt nearer than ever, and His presence was manifest. In these moments of His palpable closeness, He whispered to me His heart and His desire that I be willing to give men permission to affect me as well. I assured God that I would when the opportunity presented itself. Little did I know, less than a month later, I would be sitting in front of a vase of roses in my hotel room while this question loomed in my heart---Do I let him affect me?

During the ten minutes of staring at those roses, I had a conversation with myself. The old me and new me were battling for control of the situation. The old me knew how to pretend men didn't affect her and the new me had just given God permission to affect her deeply. Now, I knew I was being asked to do the same for a man. True change is not proven until it is tested, and this was my moment of truth.

Honestly, it was touch and go for that entire ten minutes. My first thought was: *Call him and thank him for the flowers, but stay cool, calm, and collected. Don't let him know you are excited or that you love him. Keep him guessing. Don't show all your cards.*

Quickly my second thought, coming from the new place in my heart that God was developing, followed--- *Call him and don't hide*

the gushing feeling you have in your heart. Tell him how it touched
you. Let him know how excited you are. Don't manipulate him or
keep him guessing. Let him know he affected you.

I listened to the latter and called him and poured out my joy. His
delight was apparent on the other end of the line, and I was happy
that I didn't rob him of that by being flat lined in my emotions. I
couldn't wait to see him, and made sure he knew that.

It's one thing to give God or a guileless man like Caleb permission
to affect you, but it's another thing entirely to open your heart to a
man you love and who is in love with you, especially when he is
one of your best friends. Those relationships are expensive to keep
and even more expensive to lose. That's the cost of love
sometimes. It's risky.

You may be thinking to yourself, "Tara, it would have been okay if
you were more guarded. You didn't need to show all your cards
like that." I can honestly say that may be true in some situations,
but in that moment I sensed the importance of being honest, clear,
and pure. I wanted no games from the start. I knew the
importance of "guarding my heart" as people quote from Proverbs
4:23. How many times had I heard that scripture quoted in similar
situations? Many times! I used it as an excuse to withhold my heart
from people out of fear rather than out of wisdom. Sometimes fear
masquerades as wisdom, and I wanted no part of fear.

Amid being aware of the importance of "guarding the heart", I also knew that 1 John 4:18 teaches "...he who fears has not been perfected in love." With both of these scriptures in mind, I chose to express my heart without fear while trusting God to speak to me if I needed to reel in my heart. He is really great at protecting us, which is probably why I had some questions for Him after my fiancé left.

After the engagement was broken, I often asked God the ever popular "Why" questions. One that came up time and again was: *Why would You have told me to allow myself to be affected by a man if You knew it would end with one leaving me?* That question and many more were answered as I continued to travel the path of an Overcoming Bride. You will know the answer to this question too, but I'm getting a little ahead of myself. Know that as you take this trip down memory lane with me, you will experience the path God led me on, and perhaps answers to questions about your personal journey with God.

Chapter Three

Finding God

To this day, I don't regret responding authentically, honestly, and from my heart during the entire short-lived romance. However, because of the way our relationship came to a crashing halt, that authenticity did not come without price of pain and tears. When my former fiancé left, I lost a friend who knew me since the week my mother passed away in 1999. A constant in my life from that point forward, he had weathered many seasons with me, as I had with him. I fully trusted him and couldn't wait to see what the coming years had in store for us together. Losing him was like witnessing my past, present, and future disintegrating before my very eyes.

After that painful Skype call, I immediately went downstairs where my wedding dress was hanging, and I gently took it in my arms and laid down on the floor with it. I wept for what seemed like an eternity. I begged and pleaded with God to do something about what was happening. I had hoped that within a few hours or days this nightmare would be over, and I would still be on the course to marry my best friend.

My former fiancé had requested strongly that I not try to contact him in any form because it was too painful for him, and he went off the map of my life from that point forward. That day and the next, hoping the silence would be broken, I obsessively checked my phone to see if I had missed any calls. In the weeks and months that followed, no call ever came. All I had was silence.

It's amazing how something as seemingly benign as silence can be so excruciating. Of all that I endured during that time, the silence hurt the most. Yes, I suffered through the walk of shame returning the dress to the bridal salon---bearing the weight of the fact I was officially no longer a bride. And, of course, I had to field phone calls from tuxedo rental places, the wedding venue, the bridal registry representative, the caterer, and random wedding vendors until the wedding date passed. All of these things were agonizing in and of themselves, but nothing compared to the pain of silence.

However, during this season, I am certain that even though one man was silent, Jesus was not. His eyes were on me, and I was still His bride even if I was feeling disconnected in my heart from that reality. Over the next couple of years, He would spend a great deal of time reinforcing His love for me and that He is my Bridegroom.

However, it took a while for me to comprehend exactly what that meant.

One sign that He was taking care of me during this season was that He had prepared the best place for me to grieve and heal in the aftermath of the broken engagement. I moved in with my friends Dave, Michelle, and their teenage son, Dylan. They embraced me and opened their home to me as I transitioned back into the reality of life as a single woman. Thinking I would be getting married in just a few short months, I wasn't expecting to need to look for a place to live as a single woman, so I was incredibly thankful for their hearts to be used by God in providing a place for me.

At the time I moved in, I had only met Michelle once. A mutual friend introduced us just a year before. Thus, the day I moved in, I barely knew Michelle, and I was meeting her husband and son for the first time. This doesn't sound like the easiest place to grieve and bare one's soul, but by the time I moved out less than a year later, they were family. Dave and Michelle's first spouses had both passed away nearly a decade and a half earlier, and Dylan lost his father when he was five years old. These three were no strangers to grief and loss, and they had tremendous grace for me in this season.

They lived in a beautiful home with a front porch view of every summer sunset one had time to sit and watch. One night, while sitting in a rocking chair on the porch, sipping cool water from a mason jar, and watching the sunset, my tears began to flow. Grief came like waves and interrupted even beautiful moments like this in the beginning. Tidal waves of grief would wash over me and be sucked away as quickly as they came. I was terribly afraid I would never stop crying, but I always did. It was in this particular moment of the high tide of grief that I cried out to God, "I don't see You in this season! I am looking everywhere for You, but I can't find You. You have to be here. Even in this dark night of the soul that I am going through, I must find You. I will find You."

In this raw and tender moment, I distinctly heard God whisper to my heart, "To find me in this season, you need to read the story about Mary, Martha, and Lazarus." Immediately, I searched the scriptures for this story and hoped the treasure of God's heart awaited me in it. I opened my Bible to John 11:1-44 and read the story of Lazarus' death and resurrection. Lazarus had been sick, and by the time Jesus arrived in his town, Lazarus had been dead four days. Jesus loved Mary and Martha (Lazarus' sisters) and Lazarus, and when He arrived, He was entering into a grieving town. Martha greeted Him first, and she was not a happy camper. She said, "Lord, if you had been here, my brother would not have died." Martha greeted Jesus with the concern that He was too late, and He responded with a teaching on how He would reveal His glory through resurrection.

Then, it was Mary's turn to approach Jesus, and in John 11:32, she makes the same statement Martha had made just a few moments prior. After falling at His feet and weeping she says, "Lord, if you had been here, my brother would not have died." Instead of giving Mary the same teaching Martha received, John 11:33 reveals that, "When Jesus saw her weeping, and the Jews who had come with her also weeping, he was deeply moved in his spirit and greatly troubled." After this, Jesus asked to be led to the tomb, and He wept. Shortly after, He raised Lazarus from the dead.

Both women had the same concern, but they didn't receive the same response from Jesus. They both struggled with the same questions and concerns that I had on the porch that night. I wondered where Jesus was in that moment and feared He may be arriving too late to do anything about my pain and loss. I asked Jesus this question after reading the story: *Even though Martha and Mary both expressed the same exact concern, why did they each get a different response from You? Why did one get a teaching and the other get Your tears?*

Then, I heard His same gentle whisper in my heart as I had moments earlier. He said, "Tara, one gave me her concern, but the other gave me her lament. One gave Me her questions and I answered them, the other gave Me her emotions in the core of her heart, and I responded with the core of Mine."

It was then that I realized that when God had asked my permission for Him to affect me, He was expressing only half of His desire. Knowing Him was only part of the equation. He knows me, but He wanted me to realize that I affected Him. He desired to give me all of Him, but He also wanted all of me—not just my joy and laughter but all of the other emotions too. It surprised me to know that He actually treasured the honesty of my tears and the authenticity of my pain expressed in this season.

What impact does that kind of honesty have on the heart of Jesus? As in the case with Mary, He is "deeply moved" and "greatly troubled," and He takes action on her behalf. When we hurt or experience injustice, God does not sit passively by while we suffer. He is deeply moved with compassion and begins to charge toward our loss in the same way he swiftly moved toward Lazarus' tomb to bring justice and resurrection. That resurrection may not look like a restoration of exactly what we lost, but He does pursue justice for us and His justice far exceeds what any human can offer us.

In no way am I saying that we should or even could manipulate God with our emotions. However, our emotions matter to God, and when we stuff them, hide them, or deny them, we only rob ourselves of the cleansing that our lament brings when it falls upon the heart of a compassionate God. Ultimately, when we deny our emotions, we rob God of the liquid gold of our honest tears and we rob ourselves of experiencing His validation and comfort.

After studying this passage and digging deep into the messages I sensed Jesus was teaching through it, I became aware that Jesus is way more affected by what happens in our lives than I ever realized. He not only weeps for us, but He weeps with us. In Romans 8:34, Jesus is described as being "at the right hand of God," and that He is "interceding for us." He bears our burdens so we don't have to shoulder them, and He intimately knows our pain.

This type of intercession flows from Him as He empathizes with us as our High Priest. Hebrews 4:15-16 says,

> For we do not have a high priest who is unable to sympathize with our weaknesses, but one who in every respect has been tempted as we are, yet without sin. Let us then with confidence draw near

to the throne of grace, that we may receive mercy and find grace to help in time of need.

Mary came boldly before Jesus' "throne of grace" to obtain mercy, and she received exactly that. We are invited to do the same. In the days that followed, I gave Jesus what He called the "gift of my lament." When the emotions of grief reared up on their haunches, I would bury my head in a pillow and cry, or I would drive out to a field near where I lived and languish before God. I poured out my heart and tears to Him. I wailed out the prayers of a thirty-seven year old woman who still longed to be a wife and mother, and Jesus was weeping with me and for me. His tears, however, were not tears of defeat. They were building an ocean of love around me, and they were preparing me for the actions that He planned to take on my behalf.

In a world where all humans have free will, and thus, the ability to choose to hurt or to heal others, it's comforting to know that we have a God who brings love to us when people withhold theirs. In my grief, it soothed me to know that Jesus was not only crying with me and for me, but His compassionate tears and intercession possessed a power to bring restoration in my life. That night, on the porch, the beautiful sun may have been setting behind the trees, but the "Sun of Righteousness" described in Malachi 4:2 was rising with healing in His wings around me. Amid all of my grief and pain, I felt a glimmer of strength being birthed in me, and God felt closer than I ever fathomed.

Chapter Four

Empowered in the Wilderness

I know it might sound crazy, but as I entered into this "wilderness" season of my life, the book of Job became quite an encouragement to me. Two powerful questions resounded loud and clear as I read the encouragement on those pages. These two most critical questions are found in Job 1:8 where God said to Satan, "Have you considered my servant Job?" and in Job 1:9 where Satan asks God, "Does Job fear God for nothing?"

Many people believe that in this conversation between God and Satan in Job chapter one, a cruel God is playing a big chess game with Job's life, and Job is merely a pawn in God's hand. I believe something different is occurring. Satan told God that he had been roaming around the earth, and God asked him if in all of his wanderings, he had "considered" or noticed Job. Then, God begins to brag about how Job honors Him and walks uprightly. He was proud of Job and pleased with his life. Satan, feeling threatened that a man with free will would actually choose to love and serve

God, suggests that Job is only doing this because God has provided for him extravagantly, and that if He stopped spoiling him, Job would end up acting like a rebellious teenager. Satan suggests that if God stopped blessing Job with His favor and protection, Job's reverence, commitment, and fervor would most likely cease. God, however, knows differently, and suggests that Job's reverence of Him is unconditional and pure. God knew that even if the enemy robbed from Job, Job would still love and serve Him.

What if Job's story is actually about God's confidence in His children's love for Him and not about some diabolical chess game He was playing with Satan? What if this story is more about God's reward when we choose Him above all earthly blessings? What if God had the same confidence in you or me that He had in Job? What if our love for God flowed with consistency and wasn't based on His performance meeting our standards?

All throughout scripture, in addition to Job, we see examples of those who continued to love and obey God even if that commitment had the potential to cost them their deepest desires and dreams. Abraham's deepest desire for a child came to fruition, but even that fulfilled desire failed to impede him from being willing to sacrifice his son for God. Not only was having a son Abraham's desire, that son was God's promise. Yet, as we read in Genesis 22, Abraham did not question God's goodness as he was taking Isaac up the mountain to minister to the Lord. In fact, Abraham did the opposite. In Genesis 22:8, he reassured Isaac and prophesied of God's goodness by saying, "God will provide for himself the lamb for a burnt offering, my son."

In this wilderness season of my life, I, like Abraham and Job, sensed that I had the opportunity to give God something He is worthy of---my love even when my deepest longings for my future had been stripped away. However, I was fully aware of Satan's low expectations of me. He expected my love of God to be conditional and based on my terms. It was almost as if I could hear the enemy saying to God, "There's no way Tara will serve You for nothing. She will buckle under this. God, You know her deepest desire is to be a wife and a mom. If she loses that, she will curse you." All the while, my heart was saying, "Wait, God. No! He's wrong. You are worthy of so much more than that. What is happening in my life is not your fault. I don't understand all that is happening, but I know You are with me, and I still love You!"

When we are in seasons like this, our worship and connection with God becomes like the alabaster jar of expensive ointment poured upon Jesus in Matthew 26:6-13. Here's the story:

> Now when Jesus was at Bethany in the house of
> Simon the leper, a woman came up to him with an

expensive alabaster flask of very expensive ointment, and she poured it on his head as he reclined at the table. When the disciples saw it, they were indignant, saying, 'Why this waste?' For this could have been sold for a large sum and given to the poor. But Jesus, aware of this said to them, 'Why do you trouble this woman? For she has done a beautiful thing to me. For you always have the poor with you, but you will not always have me. In pouring this ointment on my body, she has done it to prepare me for burial. Truly I say to you, wherever this gospel is proclaimed in the whole world, what she has done will also be told in memory of her.'

This woman shared in Christ's sufferings as she prepared Him for burial. Even Jesus' disciples were concerned about the cost of this worship and felt it would have been better to use the perfume in another way. However, Jesus said what she did was "beautiful" and that not only would her worship be remembered by Him for eternity, but wherever the gospel was preached, her story would be told as well.

In the wilderness seasons of my life, I have been consumed with a desire for something of value or worth to come from them, and this one was no different. I believe God gave me this desire because He fully planned to pour out His grace to ensure that it would happen. My heart's cry was that one-day I would be able to say that this momentary suffering was worth it.

Worshipping God in these times is costly worship, but it's an extravagant expression of love when we minister to the Lord in this way. Just as in the case with the woman with the alabaster jar of ointment, we have the honor of pouring out upon Jesus something of value through worship that is unforgettable and remembered for eternity. Amid the moments of excruciating grief and honesty of my emotions before God, a strength rose up in me, and I knew I wanted to prove Satan wrong, and give God something of value that is rarely poured out to Him when everything is going well. I used this opportunity to give Him the extravagance of my heart from the depths of a place in me that was split wide open in the midst of grief.

This pouring out to God is such an honor and joy, but it's definitely not easy. I desired to posture myself this way before God, but, honestly, I had no idea how to do it. Sometimes I was angry with Him and didn't trust Him. I wanted to know the answer to all the "Whys" surrounding the situation. I would wonder how I could worship a God I didn't trust, but realized the simple fact that I kept coming to Him, instead of turning away, was worship. Every time I chose Him, whether I was angry, fearful of trusting, hurting, joyful, or anywhere else on the emotional map, I was pouring expensive ointment on Him in a season with many unknowns. These types moments are the building blocks of faith. I was saying, "I don't understand this at all, but I would rather go through this with You (God) than without You."

Although I perceived my connection with God was weak many times throughout this season, He saw it as beautiful. My devotional times with God failed to be as pristine as I wanted them to be. I didn't have the candles lit, the music playing, and my journal opened. Most of the time I crumpled to the floor like a sack of potatoes and wept while telling God I just wanted to go be with Him and not endure the pain anymore. Then, He would comfort me. This same scenario would repeat multiple times a day. I felt horrible that I wasn't saying nice things to Him, and all I seemed able to muster up as an offering was my pain. But I kept showing up, and so did He. This made me love Him more every day.

When we choose this path toward extravagant worship, there is great reward. As 1 Peter 4:13 describes, when we "share in Christ's sufferings," we also get to "share in His resurrection" and in that resurrection glory, He creates beauty from the ashes in our lives but not while we passively sit back and watch. God beckons us into a partnership with Him to witness restoration come, and I felt Him drawing me closer to Him in my wilderness, so that we could experience restoration together.

These invitations to draw close in the middle of suffering, pain, or contradiction are ever-present in scripture. Remember Joseph? His story was told in Genesis 37-50. He received prophetic dreams from God about his future, and as a zealous young man, he shared those words from God with his brothers. These brothers became jealous, and Joseph quickly found himself being sold into slavery by his brothers. Not long after being sold into slavery, he was unjustly imprisoned in Egypt. It would have been easy at this point to blame God for allowing this suffering to happen in his life. Two years passed in that prison cell, but God's eyes were always on Joseph, and He never forgot the prophetic promises He spoke over Joseph's life.

While Joseph was in the prison cell, he continued to operate in his calling, and he did not forget God. While in jail, he was a developing leader while interpreting fellow prisoners' dreams in Genesis 40. Not only did he interpret their dreams, but also, he eventually found himself in front of Pharaoh interpreting his in Genesis 41. As a result of hearing God's voice, and accurately interpreting Pharaoh's dreams, Joseph was released from prison and rose to be second in command in Egypt---all because he never stopped leaning into God in a time of contradiction or loss.

What would have happened if he had lost connection with God and blamed God once he was put in prison? Would the outcome have been the same? God never forfeits His promises for our lives. However, we can forfeit those promises when we choose to completely disconnect from Him when we appear to be in a time of contradiction of what He promised. Psalm 105:19 reveals Joseph's test when it says, "Until what he [God] had said came to pass, the word of the LORD tested him [Joseph]." God's promises actually become tests in time of contradiction.

Even Jesus experienced an intense time of testing. As Luke 3 describes how Jesus experienced the spiritual rush of being baptized, feeling Holy Spirit descend upon Him like a dove, and hearing His father declare, "You are my beloved Son; with you I am well pleased." However, immediately after this, Jesus experienced the wilderness. Luke 4:1 says "And Jesus, full of the Holy Spirit, returned from the Jordan and was led by the Spirit into the wilderness." This is the way I felt in this season of my life. I was immediately ushered through a wilderness season right after I had been on one of life's mountaintops, but at least I wasn't alone---the Spirit was leading me.

One important thing I had to learn in this season was that just because the Spirit led Jesus into and through the wilderness, it did not mean the Spirit caused the wilderness. I have heard many people say that Jesus gave them cancer or some other "thorn in the flesh" to teach them faith, or that He broke their leg and put them on bed rest to teach them how to obey the Sabbath. One of the biggest plots of the enemy against us in the wilderness is to convince us to blame God for what the enemy is actually responsible for. God does NOT tempt us or inflict suffering. He is a good Father and the "Father of Lights with whom there is no variation or shadow due to change," as described in James 1:17. Therefore, God can't be anything other than good. Satan, on the other hand, is the one who inflicts suffering, and unfortunately, he often uses people and their free will as part of his plans.

I also had to keep reminding myself that during this time when I was in the wilderness, I was not devoid of God's presence. In fact, Psalm 34:18 says, "The Lord is near to the brokenhearted and saves the crushed in spirit." During Jesus' time in the wilderness, angels ministered to Him, and the Spirit of God was close by, leading Him. Thus, supernatural encounters and revelation await us in the wilderness. No matter where we are---in the wilderness or on the mountaintop---we can experience God. The wilderness is just geography. God is omnipresent!

Something else I noted about Jesus' experience in the wilderness is that it led to greater power being released in His life. Jesus went into the wilderness "full" of the Spirit as Luke 4:1 indicates, but after spending forty days there, He returned to Galilee in the "power" of the Spirit according to Luke 4:14. Our connection with God during a wilderness season produces authority and power in us as well. Just like a tree during the winter, we may not be aware of our growth or have visible fruit in the wilderness, but we will eventually experience God's increased authority and power made manifest in us and through us, if we stay connected to Him through the process.

Just like in the aftermath of Jesus' wilderness experience, others in scripture saw the same level of exponential victory. When Job came out of his wilderness, he had a justice package waiting for him, and all that he lost and more was restored to him. When Joseph was released from his wilderness in the prison, he immediately transitioned from being a falsely accused and wrongly imprisoned convict, to being second in command in Egypt. When Moses returned from forty years in the desert after killing the Egyptian, he entered his ministry of leading an entire nation out of slavery. These were the types of victories I wanted to see come from my times in the wilderness.

As each day edged closer to what would have been the wedding day, I wanted to be proactive in choosing how and where I would spend the month of August in 2013. I imagined myself waking up on August 24th wishing I could sleep through the entire weekend, or spending days depressed as I looked at the clock and envisioned what would have been happening at that exact moment in time had I been getting married.

I considered how far less than victorious it would have felt to be laying in bed all day thinking of all that could have been, and the idea of grieving for an entire weekend actually repulsed me. In this season, I felt powerless against silence, grief, and pain. Frankly, I desperately wanted to regain my power---not my soul power but God's power operating in and through my life. I sensed there were two ways I could accomplish this. One was found in ministering to God, and the other was found in ministering to others.

Knowing the importance of worshipping God and staying connected to Him in the wilderness, as well as the power that awaited me on the other side of the desert, I decided to spend the "wedding month" ministering in Thailand. I figured if I wasn't getting married, at least I could invite people to be part of the great wedding in heaven described in Revelation 19:7-9.

Chapter Five

The "Wedding Month"

Running to God instead of away from Him came natural at times and was a simple act of my will at others. Nonetheless, by God's grace, I chose to stay connected and not withhold myself from Him. Just as in the scene with the woman and the alabaster flask, that's what I considered ministry to Him---not withholding worship and connection even when it's expensive. Love may come easy at times and sometimes love is a choice. However, God knows that when we choose Him above all other options, including all earthly blessings, that is extravagant love and worship.

When I boarded the plane for Thailand, and found my seat, I wanted to do one more thing before we were asked to shut down our electronic devices. I wanted to text my former fiancé and tell him I loved him. Even amid all of the grief I was experiencing, I somehow couldn't rid my heart of love no matter how hard I tried. He was someone I had known for thirteen years, and I had more good memories of him in my heart than negative ones. It was difficult for me to define him by his actions the day he left, and God didn't want him to be judged solely because of them either. My heartfelt desire at that time was to protect my former fiancé from the pain I was experiencing, and I knew that it was quite possible his pain was even greater than mine.

Believe me, I am no super human when it comes to forgiveness. My emotions ran the gamut during this time, and my days were not devoid of anger for the way my fiancé left. I just knew that I have been forgiven and given grace from God in my own life. From past experiences, I knew that holding unforgiveness in my heart would only place me in a prison of my own bitterness.

I didn't want to be like the servant in the Parable of the Unforgiving Servant in Matthew 18:21-35. The master had forgiven his servant for a great debt, but shortly after, the servant sought out a fellow servant who owed him and demanded payment of a significantly smaller debt. The master found out about this, and he imprisoned the unforgiving servant. Because of his unforgiveness, he would remain in the cell until he paid off the previous debt he owed the master.

This parable reveals that bitterness is a pricey choice. The last thing I needed in my life at this point was a prison of my own creation, so because I couldn't forgive in my own strength, I asked

God to give me His grace to forgive early in this journey. He answered that prayer and gave me grace to extravagantly forgive in a way I didn't realize was possible.

That grace, combined with the love for a man who was my friend much longer than he had been my fiancé, compelled me to send that text before I left the country. After sending it, I shut down my phone, and tears began to well in my eyes and stream down my face. I trembled as I held back groans and cries that wanted to come forth in that moment. I was confronted with so many realities---the fact I would not be getting married as planned, the death of my desire to reconcile with a man I deeply loved before our wedding day, the fact I was on another mission trip as a single woman. I released my emotions as appropriately as I was able while the plane jetted off down the runway. That entailed pretending to look out the window while the tears escaped my eyes and pain bellowed up from my heart.

When the plane leveled out, my emotions had not. I still carried the burden of knowing that my journey in life had taken a great detour. I missed my former fiancé, and I wished he was with me. I still longed for him and felt like I left part of my heart in America.

However, I carried Psalm 126:5-6 in my heart, and received it as a prophecy over my trip. As I wept during the first hour of my flight, these verses seemed more prophetic than I ever imagined they would be. In them, the psalmist declared:

> *Those who sow in tears shall reap with shouts of joy.*
> *He who goes out weeping, bearing the seed for*
> *sowing, shall come home with shouts of joy, bringing*
> *his sheaves with him.*

I had tears, but I also had seed for sowing. I trusted and hoped joy would be on the horizon. I wanted a harvest and inheritance for God in this season. I had traveled to Thailand to minister numerous times, and I loved ministering in the red light district and among the poor. It was more than a divine distraction for me to be ministering to others during this time. I truly love the people of Thailand, and I was eager to see what God would do in the upcoming month.

Another scripture that I held in my heart for this trip was Isaiah 58:6-12. I bolded some words God emphasized to me. It reads:

> Is this not the **fast** that I choose: to loose the bonds
> of wickedness, to undo the straps of the yoke, to let
> the oppressed go free, and to break every yoke? Is it
> not to share your bread with the hungry and bring
> the homeless poor into your house; when you see

the naked to cover him, and not to hide yourself from your own flesh? Then shall **your light break forth** like the dawn, and your healing shall spring up speedily; your righteousness shall go before you; the glory of the Lord shall be your rear guard. Then you shall call, and the Lord will answer; you shall cry, and he will say, 'Here I am.' **If you take away the yoke from your midst, the pointing of the finger**, and speaking wickedness, if you **pour yourself out** for the hungry and satisfy the desire of the afflicted, **then shall your light rise in the darkness, and your gloom be as the noonday.** And the Lord will guide you continually and satisfy your desire in scorched places and make your bones strong; and you shall be like a watered garden, like a spring of water, whose waters do not fail. And your ancient ruins shall be rebuilt; you shall raise up the foundations of many generations; **you shall be called the repairer of the breach**, the restorer of streets to dwell in."

After reading this scripture in the days following my fiancé's departure, I realized there are several keys to healing in the midst of grief, but one is something that few actually like doing---fasting. However, what I sensed God asking me to fast from had nothing to do with food. He was actually inviting me to fast from my grief. What was the way to do this? Minister to others by pouring myself out. This was another way to release that precious and costly ointment upon God as well. After all, Jesus said in Matthew 25:40, "Truly I tell you, whatever you did for one of the least of these brothers and sisters of mine, you did for me."

Some use ministry, work, or just being busy as a means of denying their grief and pain. I am most definitely not talking about this kind of pouring out. The fast and pouring out to which I am referring is the kind that is done in tandem with personal grief, not divorced from it. Based on this passage, I knew that as I poured myself out in Thailand, I would experience the Healer just as the Thais would, and I longed to see my "gloom" to transition to "be as the noonday" as described by Isaiah.

I also recognized the importance of removing "the pointing of the finger" from my life. The circumstances surrounding me made that difficult but not impossible, especially with the grace of God. That grace enabled me to send that text before beginning my journey to the other side of the world, and it was the grace that would continue to overshadow me the entire trip during the wedding month.

Finally, from this passage in Isaiah, I recognized that in the midst of this "fast," I would be able to experience what it was like to be a "repairer of breach" and a "restorer of streets." I relished the fact that I didn't have to wait to leave the wilderness to begin seeing fruit come from my time there. Plus, I was aware that God, who is described as "The Lord of the Breakthrough" in 2 Samuel 5:20, would empower me to overcome as well. However, despite what is possible when we choose to pour out by ministering to God and others, grieving and ministering at the same time seemed less than ideal. At times, I wondered if I had made the right decision in going to Thailand, and I especially wondered that on the wedding day.

After many days of ministry in Thailand, the "wedding day" arrived, and I was scheduled to minister in a church that morning. I underestimated how difficult it would be to even get out of bed on August 24th, 2013. I rolled from my bed and sunk to the floor. I wept before the Lord and told Him I didn't want to be in Thailand anymore, and I'd rather be getting married. I sobbed as I kept saying, "Today was supposed to be my wedding day. I can't do this! I can't do this!" That's when I heard Him whisper, "You're right, Tara. You can't do this. But I can, and I can minister through you." I felt His comfort, but still felt the searing pain and shame of being a "widow" instead of a bride. It was then that I called my Aunt Sue and Uncle Darrell in the U.S.

My uncle reminded me of the story when Jesus was grieving the death of John the Baptist in Matthew 14:13-14. In losing John the Baptist, he lost a follower and forerunner of His ministry. He clearly had a deep love for John and described him in Luke 7:28, by saying, that there was no man born of women greater than John. John the Baptist declared Jesus' first coming and prepared the way for Him, and losing John the Baptist was a painful blow to Jesus' heart. Like the way many of us would respond in a similar situation, Jesus went away to be alone with His father.

As He was departing, a crowd needing ministry followed Him. Matthew 14:14 reveals that, "...he [Jesus] had compassion on them and healed their sick." After sharing about this passage, my Uncle Darrell began to encourage me by telling me that no one, including God, would have faulted me for staying in the U.S. surrounded by friends and family comforting me during this time. Even Jesus went away to find space to be alone when John the Baptist was beheaded. However, my uncle explained, when Jesus was grieving, He leaned into His father's compassion, prayed for a crowd and all of those who were sick in the crowd were healed. My uncle's final point was a prophecy. In his typical gentle yet authoritative way, he declared, "The same will happen for you today as you lean into Jesus. You will see God do miracles."

With those words, I rose from the heap of tissue and tears on the floor, and began to get ready for the morning church service. I called my friend, Angkhana, who had traveled with me that weekend and was sleeping in the hotel room next door. God had given me a precious woman to travel with that weekend, and she, too, was experiencing her own grief. My "wedding week" was also the anniversary of the week when her husband passed away. I asked her to join me in my room to pray for the upcoming day together. One widow, and a woman who felt like a widow, knelt on the floor by the bed, wept in each other's arms and cried out to God for His glory to be revealed that day.

Angkhana and I had traveled about four hours from Chiang Mai, Thailand to the northern border of the country just a few days before, and we were eager to see what God had planned for this little house church nestled in a close knit village. There were not just Christians at the house church that day. About forty or fifty people were squeezed into this little room, and some were Buddhists. They came to hear the foreigner speak, and they were told to expect Jesus to perform miracles. That morning I preached about the power of the cross and the shedding of God's blood. I explained why God loves healing and saving us, and then I gave God space to do both. All in all, twelve people were healed that day and two people accepted Christ.

Witnessing how God poured Himself through a widow and a woman who felt like a widow (me) choosing to pour out while simultaneously grieving, shattered all my paradigms of what we are capable of when we lean into God's grace. For the first time on this trip, I was glad I wasn't in the U.S. getting married. I was equally glad that I went to Thailand and grieved while pouring out. I was going to grieve no matter where I was, but I wanted God to get the most glory out of that grief. The enemy had won nothing in this wilderness of my life. God received two more children into His family that day, and I experienced immeasurable joy in the wilderness of my life. I may have lost a best friend, a marriage, and a wedding, but I didn't lose my relationship with God or my ministry.

When we left the house church that day, we were in the middle of a torrential downpour. I wondered if we were even going to make it to the bus station for our trip back to Chiang Mai. We did make it to the bus station, and began the four-hour journey "home." Unaware of what was about to happen upon returning to my hotel in Chiang Mai, I reclined in my seat, and drowned out all the noise around me with peaceful worship music piped into my ears from my iPod.

Soon I would be experiencing the most powerful moment of the entire trip, but the events leading up to it started before we left for the northern border. The evening before we departed for the "wedding weekend" ministry, I had decided I would get a massage. Massages are very inexpensive in Thailand, and oftentimes, there are many ministry opportunities in the massage parlors, especially near the red light district. However, I knew I would be heading into a very intense weekend, so I decided to go to a spa that wasn't located directly in the red light district. I just wanted to relax. Even though it would cost more than the massages one could get in other areas of Chiang Mai, at least at this spa, I assumed I wouldn't have to worry about what was going on in the room next door during my treatment or what had taken place in my room moments before I arrived. I was expecting an uneventful and soothing time of relaxation, but God had more on His agenda.

Upon entering the spa, my massage therapist gently guided me back to the room where I would be spending the next two hours with her. She asked me to lie face down on the mattress, which was the typical way to start a traditional Thai massage. I was thankful that she could not see my face because I cried throughout the first half of that massage. I was already feeling the burden of what was about to take place in the coming weekend, and I was afraid I would not be able to minister.

Suddenly, in the midst of my tears, God began to speak to me about the woman who was giving me a massage, and I began to pray for her under my breath. When she asked me to flip over and sit up so she could massage my shoulders, she and I talked for a moment before she stationed herself behind me to pound out the knots above my shoulder blades. Her name was "Rose" (I have changed her name to respect her privacy).

I continued to pray for Rose and talk to her until she completed my massage. Rose's English was limited as was my Thai, so it was a comical game of charades just to communicate a few things. At some point, she asked me where I was staying, and I told her the name of my hotel. This was uncommon for me because I am usually extremely careful about revealing where I am staying when I am traveling. I kicked myself for revealing my hotel to Rose, who was practically a stranger, but later I realized God would use my "mistake."

After Rose ushered me to the lobby of the spa and handed me a glass of jasmine tea, I hugged her and said "Goodbye." She bowed and smiled as is the custom in Thailand, and I did the same, but what followed was unusual. She continued bowing and smiling past what was customary, and I had the sense that she didn't want me to leave. However, she did eventually back out of the room but never ceased bowing and smiling as she disappeared into the back of the spa. After finishing my tea, I made my way back to my hotel. I never expected to see Rose again.

After returning from the "wedding weekend" in Northern Thailand, I had a thought cross my mind. As I was dragging my luggage to my hotel room, I felt like God whispered something to me. He said, "I want you to go back to that massage parlor and get another massage from Rose." I argued a bit with God because I already felt a bit guilty about spending money on a more pricey massage before leaving for the northern border a few days before, and I felt this was definitely too extravagant for a missionary to receive two massages in one week---and expensive ones at that.

Why anyone would argue with God about receiving a massage is beyond me, but I definitely resisted Him. Eventually, I relented, and after quickly putting my luggage in my hotel room, I walked to the spa. I am sure the ladies at the front desk were surprised to see me just a few days after having a two- hour-long massage, but they were more than willing to accommodate me and check to see if Rose was available to give me one that evening.

Rose was working, and lo and behold, her schedule was wide open. She was extremely excited to see me, and she explained to me in broken English that she had gone to my hotel a couple of days before, but the front desk clerk told her I was gone and wouldn't be back for a couple more days. I kept asking her why she tried to visit me at my hotel, but she would shake her head and shyly explain that she didn't speak enough English to tell me. All she could say was, "You are so kind." So, as I did during the massage a few days before, I prayed for her under my breath, but this time I was also planning how I could find out what she needed the night she came to my hotel.

After the massage was complete, just like before, I was presented with jasmine tea, and she smiled and bowed, while not wanting to see me leave. It was then that I knew that meeting her was a divine appointment and that I must find out why she came to my hotel. I feared she was in trouble and needed help.

I immediately contacted my dear Thai friend, Oh, and I told her that I sensed we needed to reach out to Rose together. Oh called Rose and scheduled a time to have lunch with her that week, but the next day when Oh called Rose to confirm our appointment and check on her, a man answered the phone and told Oh that Rose would not be having lunch with us. After bullying Oh and telling her to stop calling, he hung up. Oh said that he sounded drunk.

My mind and heart raced. I knew all too well the range of possibilities of what Rose could be enduring at that moment. Was she being trafficked? Did her possessive husband abuse her? Was she afraid for her life? Is that why she came to my hotel? I told Oh that there was only one thing we could do now. I knew that we needed to schedule another massage so that we could talk to Rose.

That was the only way to avoid detection by her husband. So, Oh and I made our way to the massage parlor for the third massage of the week.

Rose was certainly surprised to see me again. I scheduled a thirty-minute massage for me and a one-hour massage for Oh. We requested to have our massages in the same room, so once my therapist left (Rose was working on Oh), we explained to Rose why Oh and I came to see her. I told her that we were not there for a massage, but it was worth it to us to pay for an appointment to make sure that she was okay. She looked around to make sure no one would be able to hear her, and after shutting the door to our room, she whispered to Oh in Thai. I was dying to know what was going on and could barely contain myself while waiting for translation.

I asked Rose to explain to Oh why she went to my hotel a few nights before. Rose spilled her heart to us and desperately shared why she came to my hotel. She explained,

> *When you came in for your first massage, I never forgot your kind eyes and your face. I needed help and I had this sense you could help me. That's why I went to your hotel to find you a couple of days later, and that's why I was so happy that you returned to the*

spa. My husband struggles with addictions, and I am
pregnant. He recently held a knife to my throat and
threatened to kill me. When I found out that he would
not allow me to have lunch with you and Oh this week,
I lost all hope. I thought my only option was to find a
medicine doctor who could make a potion to drink
that would cause my baby to be aborted. I obtained
the potion and drank it, but I have not miscarried. The
medicine doctor said that I would miscarry within
twenty-four hours, so I returned to ask him to give me
another dose. I drank it, but it has been another
twenty-four hours and I still have not miscarried, and
I don't know why.

As she shared her story, the love of God began to well in my mothering heart and I promptly said through my translator, "I know exactly why your baby did not die. God is protecting him and God is protecting you. That is why He sent me to you three times. Jesus loves you very much, and He sees you." Right after I said this, she began to shake and cry, and Oh and I hugged her and prayed for her. I knew as we held her and prayed, God was holding us all, and the three of us were experiencing His deep and profound love together.

Our appointment time was swiftly coming to a close, so we scheduled a time to secretly meet with her a couple of days later at my hotel. Finally, Rose arrived at my hotel room. Oh and I had been eagerly awaiting her arrival. We were hoping she would have the courage to keep her appointment with us and more importantly keep her baby. Thus, when Rose arrived, Oh and I began to talk with her about options for her and the baby. Then, God told me that He wanted me to say something specific to her. He said, "Tell her that I love her deeply and that I am proposing to her tonight, and that she is my bride."

Honestly, I didn't want to minister using that metaphor. After all, I had just made it through the "wedding weekend" and my heart was pretty raw in the aftermath. However, I obeyed. I began to share with this precious woman about God's heart for her and that she was like a bride being proposed to in this moment. I told her that she could say, "Yes," "No," or "Let me think about it." She promptly and without hesitation replied in a way I didn't expect by saying, "I Do." Just like a bride on her wedding day, she was ready to commit to her Bridegroom---Jesus.

In a hotel room in Thailand, just a mere few days after the "wedding weekend," a third person was giving their life to Christ. She didn't just want to be engaged to God. Rose wanted to marry him in my hotel room that night. As she prayed to Jesus and asked

Him to forgive her of her sins, she wept and reported that as she prayed, she physically felt guilt and shame being pulled from her and said that for the first time in her life, she no longer felt guilty. That spring, she gave birth to a healthy baby boy.

I now understood the fullness of what can come from pouring ourselves out even in the midst of our own grief. When we pour out extravagantly, we sometimes forget that God pours out in response. When God responds to what we pour over Him and others, He does it beyond what we could ask for or even imagine. He raises people from the dead, performs the greatest miracles, and trades our mourning for joy.

All in all, there were at least thirty physical healings and three salvations on this trip. Three people got married because I didn't, and I would not have traded that for the world. Although I departed the U.S. "weeping and carrying seed for sowing," just as God promised, I returned home with "shouts of joy" carrying the testimonies of Rose and the miracles at the house church in my heart.

I now knew the difference between being "full" of the Spirit and having the "power" of the Spirit that one experiences after going through the wilderness. A line in the sand of my life had been drawn. Although I had much more to learn, I knew I was not devoid of God's power gained by ministering to Him and with Him through one of the most difficult periods of my life.

On the flight home, the answer to one of my "Whys" was unveiled. Why would I be led into this wilderness? The answer was in the stories of a house church touched by the power of God's healing and love, in the eyes of Rose who knew freedom from guilt and shame for the first time in her life, in the cry of a new born baby boy who was almost aborted, and in the joyful heart of a single woman who discovered the power of God's love in and through the wilderness.

Chapter Six

Leaving the Courtroom of Guilt and Shame

After that trip to Thailand, friends and family expressed that they were beginning to see a twinkle return to my eyes and a skip return to my step. I remained on a spiritual high for many months to come, and I was filled with gratitude for the victories I experienced with God. Grief slowly but surely made its way out of my life, and I moved to Austin, TX to begin a new journey in ministry.

I truly felt like I was at the beginning of the end of my journey through the wilderness, but there was something I still could not shake. The shackles of guilt and shame associated with being a rejected bride had only loosened but had not been broken. Even after having a dream where God clearly spoke to me and told me that I was not guilty in His eyes, I still felt incredibly responsible for my fiancé leaving me and disappearing out of my life.

I carried the burden of thoughts like "You must be too much of

_____ or not enough of _____, and that's why he left you."
Part of me that felt like less of a woman because of the way he left.
I reasoned that no man leaves a best friend of thirteen years and
his bride, unless she is a toxic woman. I felt unworthy of love and
undeserving of marriage. My fears and shame even spilled into my
opinion of myself as a future mother. I started believing I was a
woman whose future children would be ashamed to call "mother."
I shouldered these boulder-sized burdens until a little under a
year and a half after he left.

I knew I had not been perfect in the relationship. Who's perfect
anyway? And Satan used my imperfections against me. Lies are
only powerful when they contain enough of a twisted element of
the truth that we actually believe them. Thus, holy conviction and
diabolical condemnation simultaneously vied for my attention.
Through God's conviction I knew I had failed in some areas, but
there is an astronomical difference between knowing "I failed"
versus believing that "I am a failure." One voice in my head said I
made some mistakes. The other voice declared that I was a
mistake.

God was gracious to me in my failures, but I was pummeled with
daily accusations in my mind. I had owned more than what God
wanted me to take responsibility for in the situation. He wanted

me to acknowledge where I failed, but He never called me a "failure." Nevertheless, I carried the shame and guilt of my new identity as a failure until God showed me a side of Himself that I had never met before---Jesus as a judge.

Prior to July of 2014, I was somewhat uncomfortable with the idea of God being a judge. I had not had many encounters with judges in my lifetime, but I knew that being a defendant in a courtroom standing before a judge was not a picture of paradise. In actuality, after listening to accusations in my mind for a little over a year, I identified with being a defendant, but I had no idea who the Judge was.

As I was spending some time reading the Bible one day, I had a pressing question for God. I blurted out, "Why can't I stop feeling the guilt and shame of being a rejected bride?" I had asked this question many other times in my journey, but never received an answer. Sometimes, I think God knows when we are ready to know the truth, and He doesn't always reveal everything to us when we ask. In John 16:12, Jesus says to His disciples, "I still have many things to say to you but you cannot bear them now." Perhaps all the times I had asked this question before, Jesus remained quiet because He knew, in the throws of my grief, I would not be able to bear His answer. This time, He knew I was ready for truth because the answer came quickly and authoritatively.

He said, "You carry this guilt and shame because you think there is a jury in this case, but there is only a judge. I am the Judge. I have told you I have declared you 'not guilty', and that you are free to leave this courtroom at any time. But, you are waiting for a jury of your peers---your former fiancé---to return and tell you what I have already spoken over you. That is why you are not free, and that's why you remain in this courtroom carrying the shame of Satan's accusations and lies."

I was immediately convicted and promptly asked God what I needed to do to respond rightly in this situation. He told me the truth again, as He always does. He firmly, yet lovingly said, "Repent of your idolatry. In your heart, you valued a human being's opinion of you above My opinion of you. That is what prolonged your time in this courtroom."

Even though I was deeply convicted by His words, I never felt unloved in His presence. Truth, although difficult to hear sometimes, provides a safety and freedom that flattery never delivers. Revelation 3:19 says, "Those whom I [Jesus] love, I reprove and discipline, so be zealous and repent." A good father disciplines his children and teaches them right from wrong. God is no different. He disciplines His children because He loves them, and I definitely felt loved in that moment. When God convicts, somehow He manages to leave us feeling loved and empowered.

The shame and guilt I carried had been having the opposite effect. They left me feeling weak and unworthy of love.

As I experienced what it really meant for God's kindness to lead us to repentance, as revealed in Romans 2:4, I obeyed on the spot. As I repented of my idolatry, the burden of shame and guilt were removed from me just as they were pulled out of Rose in my hotel room in Thailand ten months before. I was completely free from guilt and shame for the first time in nearly a year and a half.

Perhaps, you too have carried the shame of your own failures. The enemy's desire is to not only drag all of us into a courtroom but to keep us there our entire life. He figures if he can burden us with all of the "shouldas," "couldas," and "wouldas" in our lives, he will paralyze us from pursuing our destiny and purpose. However, what he thinks is one of his greatest strategies against us will actually be a dismal failure, if we remember who God is as our Judge. He forgets that even though our God is a judge, He is just, and that when we accept Christ, we are part of the Judge's family. Thus, we have favor with the Judge. In His justice system, because of the blood of Jesus, we get justice we don't deserve. He cleanses us and declares us "not guilty." It's only we who choose to remain longer than necessary in the courtroom, as we continue to listen to the prosecutor (Satan) accuse us before the judge or wait for a jury of our peers to return with their verdict.

Consider Peter---one of Jesus' disciples. At the Last Supper, Jesus prophesied that Peter would deny him three times. The idea that this would even occur broke Peter's heart, but just as Jesus prophesied, Peter denied him three times. Peter must have carried a tremendous burden after he denied Jesus who was not only his Messiah but his friend.

Peter, also, must have been shocked when Mary declared in Mark 16:7 that the angel of the Lord said, "Tell his disciples AND PETER" that Jesus is alive and in Galilee. I wonder if he felt relieved to know that God still remembered his name and if singling him out in this way meant that he was forgiven. This forgiveness, that he most likely hoped for, would be confirmed later as described in John 21, when the resurrected Christ shared a meal with Peter and invited Him three times to operate in his calling and feed God's sheep. Three invitations to erase the three denials. God is deliberate in all He does.

Jesus was Peter's judge, and even though Peter failed, God's forgiveness made him not guilty. What was the result of this undeserved forgiveness? As revealed in Acts 2, Peter preached at Pentecost a mere 50 days after he denied Jesus, and over 3,000 people were saved that day. What would have happened if Peter listened to the voice of condemnation and ignored a loving and just judge who invited him to leave the courtroom of his failures and enter into his destiny? Three thousand people may have never heard him preach and entered into their own destinies in God.

Nearly a year and a half after going through a broken engagement, God was still tenderly guiding me through the wilderness and teaching me along the way. Just as with Peter, He was wiping away my failures and regrets and inviting me into adventure and romance with Him. Peter endured three days of excruciating silence before He received a message from the resurrected Christ. I carried the weight of a year and a half of silence from my fiancé, but God broke that silence by beckoning me to stop waiting for a jury to tell me what only He, as Judge, could make official. He is able to give us what people are unable or unwilling to give. He gave me forgiveness and a new identity founded on the solid fact that Judge Jesus had declared me "not guilty." Each day, I edged closer to fully believing I was a bride and always would be.

__Chapter Seven__

Does Grief Have an Expiration Date?

Six months after leaving the "courtroom," I suddenly awoke in the early morning hours of February 20, 2015. I sensed that it was God who had stirred me awake, and I was compelled to pray. Groggily, I rolled out of bed and made my way to my rocking chair. As I plopped down for my 4 a.m. unexpected time with God, Ephesians 3:14-21 was on my heart:

> For this reason I bow my knees before the
> Father, from whom every family in heaven and on
> earth is named, that according to the riches of his
> glory he may grant you to be strengthened with
> power through his Spirit in your inner being, so that
> Christ may dwell in your hearts through faith—that
> you, being rooted and grounded in love, may have
> strength to comprehend with all the saints what is
> the breadth and length and height and depth, and to
> know the love of Christ that surpasses knowledge,
> that you may be filled with all the fullness of God.

Now to him who is able to do far more abundantly than all that we ask or think, according to the power at work within us, to him be glory in the church and in Christ Jesus throughout all generations, forever and ever. Amen.

This was a familiar scripture for me because I used it as a guiding prayer for my life and ministry. This was one of Paul's prayers for the church at Ephesus, and in my times of studying this prayer, I was intrigued by the meaning of the word "know," when Paul prayed that the Ephesians would "know" the love of God and that this knowing would surpass "knowledge." Paul longed for the Ephesians to possess more than just an intellectual knowledge of God; he wanted them to experience the height and breadth of God's love. That morning, this inspired me to pray this simple prayer:

> *Holy Spirit, would You reveal to me things about the Father and Jesus that I have yet to comprehend through experience?*

I knew that knowing God was much more than something we can accomplish cerebrally, and I also was incredibly aware of the fact that I still wanted experiences to affirm what I understood in my mind about God. For example, I knew God is described as a

"Father" and a "Bridegroom," but I had yet to experience Him in the fullness of those expressions. The reality is that we could spend eternity exploring one part of God's nature and probably only scratch the surface of that part of His heart, and I felt Him drawing me to ask Him for more revelation of Himself that morning.

So many Christians mentally know what the Bible teaches **about** God, but that doesn't mean they really **know** God. The Bible is supposed to lead us into encounters with the person of Jesus Christ, not be a substitution or replacement for them. Jesus is called the "Bread of Life" in John 6:35 and the "Word" who "Became Flesh" in John 1:14. I love the word of God (Bible), but I love the "Word" who "Became Flesh" so much more.

I knew the encounters I had with God in the past were not sufficient to sustain me in the present or the future, and I didn't want to solely live off of yesterday's "daily bread." In Exodus 16, God instructed the Israelites to leave their tents and retrieve God's bread in the form of manna every morning. In the same way, Jesus admonished His disciples to ask Him for "daily bread" when He taught His disciples how to pray in Matthew 6:11.

I, too, wanted fresh daily bread. Just like the Israelites were required to leave their tents and retrieve God's bread in the form of manna every morning, I left the warmth of my down comforter on a cool February morning and made the way to my rocking chair in order to retrieve my "manna." That morning, my prayer echoed Paul's heart cry for the Ephesians. I didn't want to just have **knowledge** about God----I wanted to **experience** Him afresh, particularly as Father and Bridegroom.

What happened after I prayed? Nothing observable or tangible. A lightning bolt of God's power didn't hit me, and the angel Gabriel didn't appear with a message from heaven. Actually, it was quite anti-climactic when viewing it through the lens of my flesh. I knew, however, that Matthew 7:9 says, "Or which one of you, if his son asks him for bread, will give him a stone?". Here Jesus was implying through this rhetorical question that if we ask Him for bread, He will be faithful to provide it. As I drifted off to sleep in my rocking chair, I trusted that my prayer would be answered somehow and someday.

When I woke up a couple of hours later, I had no idea that my "someday" was going to be that actual day. The answer to my prayer would begin as I was driving to San Antonio, TX from Austin, TX to minister at an event that evening. As I was driving, I was listening to music and worshipping. A song began to play from one of my playlists on my iPod. It's a song titled "Chambers" by Catherine Mullins. This song and I had a history together. I would listen to it on repeat in the days following the broken engagement nearly two years prior, but I had not listened to it in a long time. I encourage you to Google it or look it up and listen to it yourself if you are able to before reading the next section, but here are the lyrics so you can get the idea of what it's about:

Welcome into the chambers of the King
I come in 'cause He's in love with me
With my heart beating expectantly
I run into the arms of my King

Everything else in the world fades away
As I stare into His face
The look in His eyes melts my heart
And leaves me speechless
He-He loves me
He-He cares for me

I was made to be His bride
I was created to wear the purest white
I was made for God's eternal pleasure
I was created for intimacy with the Lord

Over and Over again You sing over me
Oh Jesus Sing over Me Jesus

Over and over again You romance my heart
With your songs of love

As the song played, I began to remember the times I would weep on the floor of my room nearly two years before as I listened to it. In those moments, God would remind me that no human being makes or unmakes me a bride. He would tell me that I was His bride, even though I had a difficult time knowing what that meant anymore. As those scenes came to my remembrance, I began to thank Jesus for how close He had been when I wept on the floor while feeling like a rejected bride in those days after my fiancé left. The tears began to flow as I continued to pour out my gratitude to Him. During this moment of worship while driving down Interstate 35 toward San Antonio, I began to have an unexpected experience. Waves of a gentle heat began to bathe my heart. These waves increased in frequency and temperature until there was a permanent deep heat penetrating the core of my chest. Then, I heard God's voice loud and clear. It wasn't audible, but it was the closest to audible as I had experienced before. It was more than a whisper in my spirit, and this simple sentence reverberated throughout my entire being. He said these words:

"She's mine!"

Instantly, I knew God was making a declaration over me. He was not only making sure I knew *who* I was but He was ensuring I knew *whose* I was. In that moment, I experienced the protection of a Father and the holy jealousy of a Bridegroom declaring that I belonged to Him. I wasn't an orphan or widow. I was a daughter and a bride, and just like the bride in Song of Solomon 8:5-7, my desire was that God's love for me would be like a seal over His heart, and I believed I was permanently being branded with a deeper and ever-increasing love for Him. I shared in her feelings that she expressed when she declared:

> Who is this coming up from the wilderness leaning on her beloved?...Set me as a seal upon your heart, as a seal upon your arm, for love is as strong as death, jealousy is fierce as the grave. It's flashes are flashes of fire, the very flame of the Lord. Many waters cannot quench love, neither can floods drown it...

I returned from that ministry trip a whole new woman, and I truly was in the process of coming out of the wilderness leaning on my Beloved. I couldn't wait to see what the future held, and I was especially excited about my upcoming trip to Japan. As I was preparing for the trip, I asked God for more experiences with Him. I wanted to continue to experience His love in a fresh way before heading off to minister internationally. It was then that He asked me for something expensive.

Even though each day in the wilderness became less and less about my former fiancé or him returning to me and more about what God wanted to teach me about myself and Himself in that season, I still held onto a few memories from the time when I was a man's future bride. For example, I had the engagement photos on my computer, which included the selfie I took of me with the first vase of flowers my fiancé gave me. I also, still to that day, as hard as it is to admit, held close to my heart a few memories of that romance.

———————

One of those memories was of the day my former fiancé and I drove to a waterfall just shortly after Valentine's Day in 2013. That was the day we began to plan for the wedding and shopped for rings. However, before all the planning began, we took some time together to just take in our new romance and the beauty of nature. It was a bit chilly out, so he brought a blanket and wrapped us both in it so we could sit on a park bench and enjoy each other's company and the beautiful scenery.

As I sat in my rocking chair a little over two years since that day at the waterfall, God asked me for something costly. After asking to experience more of Him, He said, "I want to answer your prayer, but I need you to do something first." Just like the rich young ruler who told Jesus he would sacrifice anything to be a follower in Matthew 19:16-26, I said, "Anything God. You are worth it."

That's when He said, "Delete the photos from your engagement. Let go, Tara. I want you to build new memorials of times you have with Me, and I want to give you new memories and photos with others. I want you to live in the moment, not in the past." I wanted to argue by saying, "But I don't look at the photos very often" or "Can I at least save the selfie?" However, as each of the arguments passed through my mind, it became even clearer how right God was.

That selfie wasn't just a harmless, innocent photo. It glorified romance as the supreme way to feel loved, chosen, wanted, and desired. Somewhere deep down, I thought that deleting that photo would also delete how I felt in that moment when I took the photo, and I didn't want to let those feelings go. It may sound weird, but subconsciously, I was afraid that if I got rid of the memories of the roses, the feeling of being in my former fiancés arms wrapped in a blanket, or the engagement photos highlighting our love, I would never know that kind of love again. The selfie and other photos and memories had an unhealthy grip on my heart, and God knew it.

One thing I learned during my journey is that grief has an expiration date. I'm not saying that we will ever cease missing people we have lost, but the level of the power that grief has in our daily lives should wane and dissipate over time. It's actually the blessing of God that "weeping only endures for a night" according to Psalm 30:5, and I'm thankful Jesus said in John 10:10, that He came that we may "have life and have it abundantly."

I am grateful that with God's grace, the depths of grief are only temporary, and I experienced this grace long before I went through a broken engagement. In the weeks and months following my mom's death when I was twenty-three years old, I could barely function. She passed away suddenly just before I was to begin my first year teaching high school English. Every day, I would teach a class, the bell would ring, and I couldn't wait for the students to completely file out, so that I could shut and lock the classroom door behind them. I would sit at my desk and cry for the entire five minutes between classes. When the tardy bell rang signaling that there was one more minute for students to arrive at their class, I would wipe the tears from my eyes, stand up to straighten my clothes, and I would walk to the door and open it.

My students never understood why I failed to greet them outside my door in the initial days of teaching, but that changed as the school year progressed. Eventually, I was able to make it through the day without being overwhelmed by my loss, and I believed that not only would I be able to survive without my mom, I would actually be able to thrive. One key to remember is although I was beginning to live in joy again, I still missed her and always will until I see her again. I know she will be on my heart on my wedding day, and when I give birth to my children, and God is more than okay with that.

The thick shroud of grief, however, is never meant to last forever, and I contend that it shouldn't. There is a point in time when grief can become unhealthy resulting in idolatry or worship of the created over the Creator. This unhealthy kind of grief paralyzes us from fully enjoying God and our friends and family who are still alive or with us. Even though I was overcoming in many ways throughout my wilderness, underneath all that strength, I was reaching a point of unhealthy grief in some of my heart.

Even though most of my grief was gone, I still held onto the last of what I had in that long lost romance---those photos, a selfie, and memories of being wrapped in a blanket on a park bench. These memories were still vying for my attention. Every time I tried to step into the present, they were beckoning from my past threatening me and telling me that if I let them go, I would never know love like that again.

Some reading this may think God's request of me was insensitive at best and flat out wrong at worst. Some may be wondering how a God who defends widows and orphans would be "robbing" me of my right to grieve in my own way. Consider these two illustrations from my life before making a decision about God's request of me:

When the Music Ceased Playing

An elderly woman I know has been a widow for twenty- five years. She dearly loved her husband, and she has always said that she would never find anyone like him after he passed away; therefore, she chose not to marry again. One of the greatest material gifts her husband ever gave her was a beautiful organ that she still has in her home to this day. She loved playing that organ, and when her husband was still alive, he loved it when she played for him. He would come home from a busy day at work, and he would draw himself a bath. He left the bathroom door open, would ease into the tub, and shout from the bathroom, "Could you play me some music on the organ?" Then, she gladly sat at the organ and played as long as her husband soaked in the tub. This was their sweet, nightly routine.

Recently I asked her if she played the organ anymore. She told me she hadn't played much since her husband died. I asked her why, and she simply said, "Well, I guess it's because I don't have anyone to play for anymore." That answer burrowed itself in my heart and I wasn't able to pry that conversation from my mind for months. I had told my her that she could still play for Jesus and me or her friends, and, before moving on to another topic, she said that she would play for Jesus in heaven one day. That Christmas, I ordered her a CD set of hymns played on a pipe organ. Even though she chose not to play the organ for anyone else, at least someone could play for her.

Sadly, for twenty-five years her grief had stolen so much real estate in her heart that she didn't even realize that Jesus loved hearing her play the organ even more than her husband did. She has always loved Jesus, but her capacity to feel and experience His love in its fullness was diminished because of her grief that was long past its expiration date. She will play the organ again in heaven one day, but my prayer is that she won't wait until then. God loves marriage and romance. After all, he created it. However, if it doesn't have its rightful place in our heart, it robs us of the precious treasure of the fullness of a connection with a loving God.

When Grief Becomes Honor

Remember my friends Dave, Michelle, and their son, Dylan? The one's who blessed me by allowing me to live with them and sit on their porch looking at those amazing sunsets. Both Dave and Michelle lost their first spouses, one to a horse accident and the other to heart failure. Michelle became a single mom to Dylan and Dave became a young widower. Neither of them had anticipated this life curve ball.

One thing I really appreciated about Dave and Michelle was that they understood grief, but they also understood how to live past the grief. They were where I eventually wanted to be. I have known people who have lost a spouse and witnessed how they immediately removed every possible memory of them from their life---including pictures. They chose to forget their spouse completely because they couldn't handle the grief. This was not so with Dave and Michelle.

One day, I happened to be in Dave and Michelle's office at the house, and I noticed something precious. Two photos of people I had never met were framed and prominently displayed on the bookshelf. One of them was of Donna Beth, Dave's first wife, and the other was of Denny, Michelle's first husband and Dylan's father. Another photo picturing Dylan and Denny stood on the same shelf. Michelle and Dave unashamedly still remembered and honored their previous spouses. However, never once did I see this honor diminish their love for God or for each other.

I knew the difference between photos that can be kept and photos that shouldn't be kept. Mine were the kind that chained me to the past and caused me to fear my future. Dave and Michelle's were the kind that honored God's goodness in the past, but acknowledged that He was doing the same in the present---Dave and Michelle's picture as well as a family photo of Dave, Michelle, and Dylan were prominently displayed on that shelf, too. These pictures honored a God who loves marriage, the widow and widower, and the orphan. They were nothing like my selfie or engagement photos, and God graciously waited two years to tell me. He knew when I was ready to embrace the truth and completely emerge out of any grief that would eventually become unhealthy.

Unlike Dave and Michelle's photos, these items I clung to---the selfie, the engagement photos, the memories--- were memorials I was now building to a god of romance instead of ones of honor like those that were lovingly placed on the bookshelves of Michelle and Dave's office. I had held tightly onto memories of human romance when all along a loving God was eagerly waiting to romance me Himself. He knew that at this point, if I continued to struggle to hold onto the fading memories of romance, my arms, and more importantly, my heart, would have less room for Him.

Some may say, "Tara, you were grieving. It had only been two years. It's okay. Everyone grieves at their own pace." I agree with them to an extent. There's a reason God didn't tell me to let go of these memorials in the early stages of my grief, but it had now been two years, and God knew what my future held and how these memorials would keep me from it. It was His love that was inviting me to follow Him and thereby not let my past continue to haunt my present and future in any way. Egypt often looks great from the wilderness, but God wanted a promised land for me, and it was time to start moving toward that land. It was time to leave this wilderness once and for all.

Chapter Eight

Buying Gold

What God was asking of me that day was expensive, but what He planned to give me in return was priceless. I simply had to make room for Him to do that. Those photos on my computer and the memories attached to them needed to make way for new photos and memories and especially the ones with God.

Sometimes when we make a request of God as I had done when I asked to have more experiences with Him the day I drove to San Antonio, TX, He gives freely without asking anything of us. He surprises us by showing up in our car and touching our hearts with the warmth of His presence. However, there are other times when He asks us to make a sacrifice first before fulfilling the desires of our heart. In Revelation 3:18, God admonishes the church of Laodicea by saying,

> I counsel you to buy from Me gold refined by fire, so that you may be rich, and white garments so that

you may clothe yourself and the shame of your nakedness may not be seen, and salve to anoint your eyes, so that you may see.

Notice, God did not say, "Come get gold." He said, "Come buy gold." I knew that God asking me to delete the photos was an invitation to "buy gold" from Him, and that I would not be disappointed. I opened my computer and made my way to the folder of photos memorializing my temporary romance. One by one, I erased each photo from the folder. Surprisingly, I didn't cry much. That was until I reached the selfie of me and the vase of roses. That was the most expensive capture of that time period to wipe out. I took it the night I returned to my hotel and saw that vase of roses. I texted that photo to friends and family, and we celebrated my blossoming romance. It represented the beginning of something, and now it represented the ending. It was difficult to let it go, but after I did, I released my short lament to God.

I was crying tears of sadness, but those tears quickly shifted to tears of love. I kept telling God that He was worth this small sacrifice. I wanted all of Him, and I knew that no one ever had or ever could love me in the fullness that He does. I knew my future husband would do his best to love me like Jesus, and, I would do the same for him. Yet, I knew that I should never expect him to be my God, and he should never expect me to be his. Thus, once again, during this journey, God removed the tentacles of the past that were strangling parts of my heart, but just as in the "courtroom" of my shame and guilt, He was about to replace them with something so much better---His love.

Just a few short moments after deleting the photos, there was a knock on my bedroom door. It was later in the evening, and I wasn't expecting company. When I opened the door, my friend Glenda was standing in front of me. I was completely and utterly surprised to see her. She lived in Los Angeles, California, and I lived in Austin, Texas, so I definitely was not expecting to see her at my door.

I was still wiping tears from my eyes as I hugged her and welcomed her. She began to explain to me that she had flown that day to Austin because God told her to minister to me before I left on my ministry trip to Japan (I was leaving in a couple of days on a one-month mission trip). I was shocked, and intrigued by the timing of this visit. I had not talked to her in a while, and she definitely had no idea about what I had just done moments before she arrived.

Glenda went on to explain that God had told her to do three things for me, and she asked my permission before she began to go through God's list. I was on the edge of my seat with excitement. It was then that she reached around the corner to pull a bouquet off of a shelf, and she handed them to me. She said, "God told me to get you flowers from Him." My heart was undone. I could barely contain myself. Jesus, my Bridegroom, was romancing me, and He was using my friend Glenda to demonstrate His love.

As I recovered from the emotions surrounding such a precious gift from God, Glenda produced the second gift. She said, "While I was on the plane, I asked God if He wanted me to give you anything else besides flowers. That's when He said that He wanted me to get you a blanket and wrap it around you when I gave it to you." Glenda thought this gift was odd, and being a new friend, she did not know me well, and she wondered if I would think it was weird that she was doing this for me. Regardless of her thoughts, and not knowing how great of an impact the second gift would make on me, she simply obeyed God.

I was completely on emotional overload at this point. I stood in utter amazement and shock as Glenda wrapped the blanket around me. God was literally reproducing for me the very things He had just asked me to delete on my computer. He was immediately making new memories and memorials with me to replace the old ones.

The third gift God gave me through Glenda was a prayer. As Glenda wrapped the blanket around me, she gave me a hug and prayed the only words God told her to pray which were "God, please remove from Tara any last ounce of grief that she experienced as a result of being a *rejected bride* and send her to Japan as a *bride.* Please wash her of any residual grief that is still trying to cling to her."

I gave God my last bit of grief that night, and He gave me His extravagant love. I released to Him my memorials built in honor of romance, and He showered me in a very personal way, with sweet surprises. He expressed His love for me with the same actions of my former fiancé---He gave me flowers and wrapped me in a blanket. The only difference is that when He gave me these gifts, just like on Calvary, He did it with full commitment in His heart, and I knew He would never leave me. He would be with His bride in Japan and always, and I was about to see how true this really was.

After being romanced by God and experiencing a refresher course in His love for me, I departed for Japan with a message burning in me. I continued ministering along the same theme I carried in my heart when I was there seven months earlier in August 2014. The message to the churches and the people of Japan was: "You Are Not a Rejected Bride." However, unlike my trip seven months before, on this trip to Japan in March 2015, I was carrying that same message but not the same weight from being a rejected bride. I would now be preaching that message as a bride, not a rejected one. In August in 2014, that message was a message in faith, now this faith message was combined with the fresh power of my experience with my Bridegroom.

In order to fully explain how God beautifully and strategically orchestrated ministry on my March 2015 trip to Japan, I need to take you back to the trip I took in August 2014 and tell the story of a Japanese man (I'll call him "Paul") who I met on one of the trains. After ministering that evening, Maiko (my dear Japanese friend and translator) and I were traveling back to her town. At one of the stations, Paul boarded the train and sat across from us. Right when he sat down, I had a random thought flash through my mind. The thought was a three word Japanese phrase----*Jin Shin Jiko*.

Anyone who lives in Japan knows about *Jin Shin Jiko*. It means "death by body," and it's how the Japanese people describe a particular way people commit suicide in Japan. Japan has one of the highest suicide rates in the world, and it is a daily occurrence (often multiple times a day) for people to jump in front of the trains as a way to end their life. This suicide method is commonly called "*Jin Shin Jiko*," and it is announced in the train stations when it happens so that people know their trains will be delayed.

When these words came to mind as Paul entered the train, I felt a sense of urgency to do something, but I had no idea if what I was discerning or hearing was even God's voice in my thoughts. I wondered if what I was sensing had something to do with Paul. I leaned over and whispered to Maiko what I sensed God had whispered to me, and she asked me what I thought we should do. I assumed we needed to say something to him, but I knew it was culturally unacceptable to talk to strangers on the train in Japan. I was also aware that Jesus didn't spend his time on earth trying to be culturally sensitive everywhere He went. He wasn't purposefully rude, but if a Samaritan women needed living water, He was going to talk to her whether society thought it was appropriate or not, and if someone needed healing, He didn't check his calendar to make sure it wasn't the Sabbath (See John 4 and Luke 13:14).

I told Maiko we needed to talk to Paul, and she asked me what to tell him. My clumsy evangelist self said without really thinking, "I don't know. Just tell him he's on the right train." I figured if he was suicidal and needed help, he was most likely on the right train because we were there to show God's love to him. Then, I added, "Tell him Jesus loves him, there's hope, God has a purpose for his life, and tell him to not give up." I simply suggested saying things that someone might want to hear if they didn't want to live anymore.

Maiko quickly stepped over to where Paul was sitting and began to share those words of life with him. She then handed him a church bulletin and invited him to church. I thought to myself---that church bulletin will probably find its way to a garbage can on his way out of the train station, but hopefully he will feel loved by God tonight.

Maiko returned to the seat next to me, and I thought our work was finished. We had obeyed God, and possibly this man's suicide had been averted. That's when another thought came to mind. I sensed God wanted me to do something that was a little more unconventional than just talking to a stranger on the train. He said: *Your work is not finished on this train. Whenever this man looks up at you during the rest of the train ride, I want you to smile at him, look into his eyes, and ask me to release My life and joy into Him.*

I thought God had literally lost it. I argued with Him in my heart, and tried to explain that this man would think I was crazy or flirting with him or BOTH! I was starting to like the idea of just handing him another church bulletin at this point, but I obeyed God even though His words did not make sense to me at all. The man did not get off the train for at least ten minutes, but every time he looked up at me, he would find me smiling as I prayed for him under my breath. Eventually, he arrived at his stop and got off the train. I assumed that I would never see him again.

When I returned to the U.S. in September of 2014, I received a message from Maiko in Japan, and she told me this man actually came to church. I was shocked. He kept the church bulletin and my smiley staring didn't scare him off. I told Maiko I wanted to meet with him for lunch the next time I ministered in Japan, so we made sure when I returned to Japan in March of 2015 that lunch with this man was part of my itinerary.

I was the keynote speaker for a conference in Tokyo, and Maiko and I scheduled to have lunch with him before we ministered at the conference that evening. As I entered the restaurant, he and Maiko greeted me. With tears in his eyes, he stood up from the table, and embraced me instead of doing the customary bow of Japan. He began to say "Thank You" in Japanese repetitively.

I had no idea at this point what he would be thanking me for, but I wanted to tell him what happened to me on the train and why we talked to him. So, I shared my side of the story, and then he asked me, "Do you want to hear my side of the story?" And, of course, I did! I was delighted there was a side to his story, and while on the edge of my seat, I listened to his testimony. Stopping multiple times when he got too emotional to get his words out, he shared the depths of his pain and the heights of hope he received that night on the train.

Several years before he met Maiko and me, his girlfriend of many years had passed away. He explained that he had woken up one morning, and she had passed away in the middle of the night next to him in bed. Around that same time, he had started a stressful job, which remained stressful throughout the years before he met Maiko and me.

Through tears and while trembling, he told us that every day since his girlfriend passed away, he considered suicide. He would even go online to research ways to end his life. That was until he met us on the train. All those years, he had been traveling the same route to work, and he had never gotten on the wrong train when going to work, but the night he met us, he had gotten on the wrong train. So, when Maiko told him that he was on the right train, it got his attention.

Isn't God amazing? The same God who was in the middle of teaching me that He pursues me as His bride was pursuing this man in Japan in the same way. He forgot no detail and He was drawing this man into relationship with Him.

He further shared that he appreciated the words we shared, but there was something else that happened on the train that he would never forget. He said that when he looked up and saw me smiling, something began to change in him. He said that all the suicidal thoughts and depression were leaving him and from that day forward, he never contemplated suicide again.

What happened to him that night on the train? He encountered a Heavenly Bridegroom who loved him deeply, and God used His bride (me and Maiko) in that process. When I first met him on the train in August of 2014 (seven months before our lunch together) I had not fully come out of the wilderness. However, Paul still saw the joyful face of a bride who was loved, and in the process of coming out of the wilderness "leaning on her beloved" (Song of Solomon 8). God's love and joy flowing through this bride was powerful enough to wipe out chronic depression and suicide.

Seven months later, in March of 2015, the Bridegroom's love flowing through His bride again led to something even greater. Two days after that lunch meeting, Paul, who seven months earlier was in the pit of despair and hopelessness, attended the Tokyo conference where I was the keynote speaker. That night, he gave his life to Christ, and now, he too, was part of God's glorious bride.

Before this moment, he had no idea that there was any love greater than the romance he had with his girlfriend. Japan is less than 1% Christian, and the closest love to God's love that many experience in Japan is romance. Yet, Paul is proof that there is a greater love than romantic love, and it's found in Jesus. Without his girlfriend, Paul, hopeless and suicidal, boarded a train bound for work in August 2014. Little did he know at the time, but God was about to show Him that a love greater than romance would empty him of despair and heal his broken heart just as God had healed mine.

Chapter Nine

Overcoming Bride

Being the bride of Christ is not defined or determined by gender. I, as Jesus' bride, was pursued and romanced by a loving God the night Glenda showed up with flowers, a blanket, and her precious prayers. Paul, the man on the train in Japan, was chased and romanced by a God who knew His deepest need and what train he needed to be on that night. Being a bride is about being chosen, wanted, and desired. Whether we are male or female, we all can identify with the desire to experience what it feels like to be pursued by this kind of love.

I understand that those who are reading this book will all be in different stages of their journeys to being an Overcoming Bride. Perhaps, you are like I was at the beginning of my journey, feeling like an orphan or a widow. Or, maybe you have believed or followed Jesus for many years, but have yet to experience the depths of His love. Maybe you are like "Rose" in Thailand and you are desperate for help and you feel like you have no one to turn to.

Maybe you are married, and all that you had hoped to find in human romance has still left you lacking the deeper love you have always longed for. Or, you could be just like the Japanese man on the train---unaware that there was any romance greater than what you have been able to experience through another human being.

No matter what leg of the journey you are on, Jesus is walking alongside you, and drawing you toward *experiences* in Him that you never thought were possible. The heart behind this book is that my victories will lead to victories for you too----one of the most important victories being the fulfillment of being complete in God's love for you. From one Overcoming Bride to another, know that you have the same invitation that I had when my fiancé left--- the invitation to find a love greater than any human being can provide. This love is only found in Jesus. He is the one who makes us all an Overcoming Bride.

Some may have expected this book to end with a story that God brought me a husband and redeemed all that I lost. I am still single, but I do have a Husband and His name is Jesus, and all my deepest longings are satisfied in Him and through Him. I believe I will one day have the joy of romance with a man again, and I will cherish him as a precious gift from God. With Jesus as my Bridegroom, however, my future husband will be free from my expectations that he be perfect or satisfy every desire in my heart (there are some desires only Jesus can fulfill). I know that because of this journey, he will gain a bride who is so much more radiant than the one my former fiancé left, and that's because I learned of my identity as Jesus' bride before I became his bride (even if you are married already, you can still learn to be Jesus' bride and it will only enhance your marriage).

I sensed that the best way to end this book was with a prayer. If you have felt compelled throughout this story of my journey to ask God to experience Him in the depths of your own heart, I invite you to pray this prayer that I wrote specifically for Jesus. It contains pieces of my heart's cry to Jesus throughout my entire journey. You may want to have a journal nearby since God may speak to you as you pray. After the prayer, I have provided ways to stay in touch with me as you continue on your journey with God.

Prayer

Jesus,

I need you! All of earth's greatest blessings pale in comparison to the beauty I have found and have yet to discover in You. Please forgive me for the times I have tried to satisfy my longing to be desired, wanted, and chosen in ways that are not pleasing to you. Please forgive me for expecting my spouse/future spouse or others to be what only You can be for me. I no longer want to value the created above You, the Creator.

I invite You to come into my life and to affect me in the depths of my soul and spirit. I am finished being in control, and I choose to forgive those who have disappointed me and failed me. I ask you to give me the same grace to forgive that You demonstrated on the Cross.

Instead of looking to humans for my justice, I turn to you, Judge Jesus, to not only define **who** I am, but remind me of **whose** I am. I turn to you to give me a justice that is far greater than any human can provide me. I am no longer looking for a jury to return to give me what You, as the perfect Judge, have already given me.

I know that You and only You are able to make beauty from the ashes in my life, and I ask You to help me to partner with You in that process. I refuse to sit passively by hoping for the best in my life. I ask you to show me how to connect honestly and intimately with You, so that I can be an Overcoming Bride.

(PAUSE HERE TO LET HIM SPEAK TO YOU---He often speaks by giving thoughts, pictures, dreams, etc. WRITE DOWN WHAT HE SAYS)

Jesus, I ask you to reveal to me if there is any expired grief in me that needs to be removed and show me if there is anything in my life that resembles Tara's selfie. I no longer want my past to have a hold on me. Show me any memorials that need to be torn down to make room for the present and future that You have for me.

(PAUSE HERE TO LET HIM SPEAK TO YOU---WRITE DOWN WHAT HE SAYS)

Jesus, I invite you to stretch out inside my heart and make Yourself at home. My heart is Yours and You alone I worship. Thank you for your forgiveness. I am thankful for You as Bridegroom. Set your love for me as a seal upon Your heart as I set my love for You as a seal upon mine right now. I pray as Paul did in Ephesians 3--- I want to know You through experience, not just knowledge.

Holy Spirit, I ask You to reveal to me things about the Father and about Jesus that I have yet to comprehend through experience.

Amen

I would love to hear from you! You can keep in touch with me via a special website developed just for Overcoming Bride--- www.overcomingbride.com. You may also visit www.tarabrowder.com for more information on my ministry, speaking itinerary, and other media available from Tara Browder Media.

Many blessings on your journey with God!

Tara

Also fromTara Browder Media:

*Available from tarabrowder.com, Amazon.com, and other online and retail outlets

What if God's voice is seldom actually a voice but more like a thought or idea He plants like a seed into our minds and hearts? Are there times we have actually already heard Him and we dismissed His voice because it wasn't loud enough or it sounded too much like our own voice? Could it be that, as in the case of Elijah, He is asking us to look for Him beyond the fire, wind, or earthquake to find HIS WHISPER?

In the first half of When God is in the Whisper, follow Tara Browder's journey in learning how to perceive and obey God's whispers. Then, in the second half, receive practical tools for *your* journey in recognizing God's voice and stepping into adventures with Him that will be beyond anything you could ever dream.